Jackie Stories

ALSO BY WILLIAM KUHN

Democratic Royalism:
The Transformation of
the British Monarchy, 1861-1914

Henry & Mary Ponsonby:
Life at the Court of Queen Victoria

The Politics of Pleasure:
A Portrait of Benjamin Disraeli

Reading Jackie:
Her Autobiography in Books

Mrs Queen Takes the Train:
A Novel

Prince Harry Boy to Man:
A Novel

Jackie Stories

Eight Friends

of

Jacqueline Kennedy Onassis

William Kuhn

Montgomery Street Press

for Bradford Brown

Table of Contents

Introduction

If a collection of books is a good guide to someone's tastes and interests, then you might think of a collection of her friends as a history of her affections. These are stories about meeting the friends, unusual acquaintances, and people who knew Jacqueline Kennedy Onassis well. The longest one is the first of eight. It's an account of my contacts over a decade with Jackie's friend from boarding school, Nancy Tuckerman. Following this are shorter pieces that describe others of Jackie's friends. They may have played a smaller role in her life than Nancy Tuckerman did, but all of them were like Nancy in having had some sort of unusual relationship with her. In one case it's an account of a work colleague with whom Jackie's relations were pleasant on the surface. Underneath the two women were quietly rivals and polite antagonists.

I was in touch with most of them a decade ago when I was writing a book about Jackie in publishing. There was no room in *Reading Jackie: Her Autobiography in Books* for everything these people told me about her. My priority was the stories of the books she edited. I often had to leave out things about her that her friends revealed to me. I stayed in touch with a handful of them after the book was done. I learned more about Jackie from them, over time, than I had in the run-up to the first book's publication.

This is mainly unpublished material that I've written up here for the first time. I've taken my rough notes from interviews and phone calls to make them into a narrative of what it was like to talk with Jackie's friends. These were all remarkable people, but not all of them have household names. Often, they were as fascinating in their own right as Jackie was. Among them was a woman who created iconic fashion images, a novelist as precise as Edith Wharton on the subject of social class, and the former chair of one of America's premier dance companies. I met them in a gentleman's club and in a high-rise apartment painted all black. I saw them over soup at a Connecticut inn and in a London apartment carved out of a former hotel ballroom. Writing up these notes, coupled with new research about the people who talked to me, has made me change what I think about Jackie herself.

The picture I now have of her is more critical than the one I had before. Occasionally she appears more cruel and less reliable than she did previously. A number of her contacts questioned her generosity. She seems sometimes less grateful for the work other people had to do to keep her going than she ought to have been. Time's passing makes possible a new detachment about her and allows for a more honest assessment. If she's more imperfect here than she was in my previous book, she's also more human.

Not all of these people were her closest friends, but in almost every instance, their relationship extended over time. They knew her well enough to see the insides of her houses. They sat down to lunch or a drink or dinner together. If they also worked on books together, they did so within the context of something more than just a business relationship with one another. Sometimes they worked for years on books that were never published. In many cases these people have now died, but in some others, I've been able to be in touch with them again, or with people who knew them, for new material.

It may also be inevitable with the passage of time and the deaths of people who had firsthand recollections of her that a historical figure's attractiveness should grow dimmer. Nevertheless, any woman who was able to put together a group of friends like this would have reason to be proud. If her legacy is partly in what she did at the White House, in the preservation of Grand Central Station, and in the hundred books she edited, it is also written legibly in her friendships. In revisiting my interviews with these people, I'm aiming to tell you something about Jackie that you didn't know before. As I worked on saying something new about her, the sketches and vignettes I was writing turned up unexpected finds. When I started I had my eye on Jackie herself, but these people who knew her were often as worthy of close attention as she was. They all left strong impressions on me. I often left them envying or admiring some part of their personality that I could never match. When seen side by side with each of them, Jackie occasionally diminishes and sometimes grows in stature, but she always looks different than she did before. If I appear in these stories too, it's a good idea for you to know a little about me in order to evaluate for yourself the conclusions I've drawn. You might have decided differently yourself.

1 A Boarding School Friend

I was in my kitchen in Chicago. The year was 2008. I was surrounded by ugly wooden cabinets from the 1970s that I'd long intended to replace. I hadn't gotten around to it. I had an important call to make. The woman I was about to talk to would be an important source, maybe the most important source, for a book I was writing. I didn't trust my cellphone's reception so I pressed in the digits of her number on my landline, which had a long, corkscrew cord attached to a phone mounted on the kitchen wall. I was pacing back and forth as I began to hear the phone on the other end begin to ring. I'd already exchanged voicemail messages with her several times. I had no idea what her life was like at the other end of the line, except that she was eighty years old and living in western Connecticut. I didn't know what to expect.

I did know that she was the friend, the colleague, the secretary, and the assistant of Jacqueline Kennedy Onassis over seven decades. They first met as schoolgirls at Miss Chapin's in New York and they roomed together in high school at Miss Porter's in

Farmington, Connecticut. She served as one of Jackie's bridesmaids when she married JFK in 1953 and ten years later followed her to the White House as her social secretary. She returned to New York with Jackie after the assassination and went to work at Olympic Airlines when she married Aristotle Onassis. After Onassis died, Nancy Tuckerman worked in an office next to Jackie's at Doubleday, one of the two major publishers where Jackie was an editor during the last twenty years of her life. When Jackie died, Nancy was one of the beneficiaries of Jackie's will.

I was then fifty-one and working on a commission from Doubleday. I was writing the story of the books she'd edited. I was the first person Doubleday was allowing to write about Jackie as their former employee. I intended to focus on her books in order to examine her tastes, her interests, and her instincts as an editor. I'd been trained as an academic historian. I'd previously written books on the Victorian monarchy and nineteenth-century politics in Britain. This was to be my first book on a twentieth-century figure for whom most of the major sources were still alive. I left my job teaching history at a small liberal arts college in Wisconsin to spend full time on the Jackie project. This was my first outing beyond academia. I was going to talk to her friends and former colleagues. I'd need to learn how to do it on the fly. If I expected anything from the call, it was that Nancy Tuckerman might be the American equivalent of one of the queen's ladies-in-waiting in Britain. These were polished women of about the queen's age, and from a similar social background, who handled some of her correspondence. They often served as her companions when she left the palace. I imagined Nancy might be someone like that.

The phone continued to ring. I wondered after about the sixth ring whether it was time to hang up even though it was the time we'd agreed to talk. Then, she suddenly picked up the phone. I said hello and introduced myself.

"How ya doin'?" she said.

Her accent threw me off balance. I wasn't sure what to say. I was to learn later that Nancy had a variety of voices and that this country friendliness was a little like Jackie's whisper. It was a ruse. It was a mask. It was meant to disarm people she was meeting for the first time. Neither of them used these voices all the time. Nevertheless, Nancy used her down-home formula on other people besides me. Her twang also surprised a *New Yorker* writer who interviewed her in 1995, the year after Jackie died.

Most of the time Nancy didn't sound like that. She had the uninflected voice and the plainspoken vocabulary of my parents' generation. Born in 1928, she was the same age as my mother and two years younger than my father. Americans who came through the Second World War as they did, having witnessed so much history, tended to speak with a modesty, a lack of exaggeration that is unlike the speech of subsequent generations. Nancy was like that too. She could occasionally slip into a Long Island lockjaw where Florida was *Floridar* and idea *idear.* Sometimes she sounded like Thurston Howell III from *Gilligan's Island*, but not often.

On that particular morning she told me she hadn't received the list of Jackie's books I'd sent her. That was to have been the basis of our conversation. I wanted to know what Nancy could remember about the different book projects Jackie had worked on at Doubleday. Without it, all we could talk about were a few general recollections. She said she didn't think she'd be much use anyway. She had helped Jackie with more personal business. Jackie had assistants like Shaye Areheart and Scott Moyers who helped with the publishing business. I sensed that she didn't really want to talk to me. There had been more than a dozen full-scale biographies of Jackie published before my book and Nancy hadn't agreed to help with any of them. She recorded an oral history of her White House years for the Kennedy Library. Other than that, she'd mostly kept her silence. She wasn't thrilled about making an exception for me.

Nevertheless, my editor was an important person in her own right. Nan Talese had a considerable reputation in the world of publishing and beyond. She telephoned Nancy and asked her to speak to me. I later found out that two of Nancy's former Doubleday colleagues also phoned her out of the blue about my book. If she was feeling at all friendly toward me, it was because she liked hearing from these people. She liked being remembered. She was ready to take a few calls from me in order to say what she could about Jackie's books, but she warned me in advance it would not be much.

There was more than a month between that call and the next time we spoke. She was traveling. She told me she was going on a cruise. She was flying to Venice. At last the list of Jackie's books turned up in her mail and she was ready to talk about it. The odd thing about our second call was that, despite her initial reluctance, she was ready to tell me two important things about Jackie. The problem was, and this was partially my own inexperience, I wasn't yet ready to hear them. What she had to say didn't fit into my pre-conceived notions of what Jackie was like, and what their relationship to each other must have been. It's only now that I'm aware of how revealing she was being. It's only now that I'm conscious of the ways I misunderstood her at first.

It started with my saying that at Doubleday Jackie had done an unusually large number of books on Tiffany and Company. There were five, among them a Tiffany cookbook, a Tiffany wedding guide, and a Tiffany book on table settings. Nancy doubted this. "That doesn't seem like her style to me." Yet, I had a small volume, privately printed at Doubleday after Jackie's death in 1994, that attributed all these Tiffany books to her. I also had the recollection of John Loring, Tiffany's former design director, that he and Jackie had worked on these books together. Why would Nancy doubt that?

She said the Tiffany books weren't Jackie's passion. She preferred things of a scholarly nature. She liked doing a book of photography on the nineteenth-century photographer, Eugène Atget. She liked acquiring the books of the Egyptian Nobel

Prize winner, Naguib Mahfouz. She liked laying out the photographs for an exhibition catalogue at the Metropolitan Museum of Art, *In the Russian Style*. I tripped up on Nancy's word "scholarly." I'd been an academic all my life. My father was also an academic. I knew scholarship as rarefied knowledge, painstakingly acquired, usually by deeply unglamorous people, and shared only with a few experts who spoke the arcane language of a discipline's specialty. It was the opposite of what I expected of Jacqueline Kennedy Onassis. I expected her to be daily distilling the essence of manners and of visual style into dozens of different book commissions. Tiffany's fit my image of what she must have been like. A photographer known for his street scenes in the era of World War I did not.

Nancy was trying to tell me this. There was a side of Jackie that liked jewels and parties, but intellectually, in the second half of her life, she aspired to be something much more than a partygoer or a president's widow. She wanted to be a connoisseur. She wanted to have the knowledge of a collector. She wanted to possess specialized insider familiarity with the arts and literature. She wanted to do the equivalent of amassing the Horace Walpole collection which her distant relation Wilmarth "Uncle Lefty" Lewis had given to Yale.

Whereas I, who'd seen the inside of colleges and universities since I was little, knew that Jackie Onassis could never fit into that world. She wasn't nerdy enough for it. She started too late. She'd never acquire the scholarly habit of shutting herself away in a library month after month. Nor could she ever be a respectable scholar if she tried to do Mahfouz *and* Atget *and* historic Russian costumes. She had to do just one and spend decades doing that alone. So if Jackie liked things of a scholarly nature, she was never going to be anything close to a scholar herself. She was always going to be outside with her nose pressed against the glass.

Nevertheless, that was what she wanted. She set aside most recollections of her White House years and chose not to think about them. Nor did she much respect rich women who rode around New York in limos. If anything she would probably have been pleased eventually to be known for her book list, although she mostly took pains to conceal the books she was working on as she edited them. She was on the road to acquiring an admirable list, but she came to her career too late, and died too early, to have made that cultural mark. She'd always be famous for the assassination, her clothes, and the Greek marriage. Those were things she'd have sooner forgotten.

I was attracted to Jackie's style and *savoir faire*. I thought of the Tiffany books as a natural extension of her public persona. What it took me a while to grasp was that those big, coffee table books were money spinners for both Tiffany and for Doubleday. They reinforced Tiffany's reputation for luxury goods. Many of the items featured in the books were on sale in the stores. It was cheaper to buy a book than it was to buy the plates in the table settings or the jewels for the weddings. Doubleday assigned these books to Jackie as the price she had to pay for the privilege of editing the high culture, smaller sales projects she preferred to do. She was working with the Tiffany marketing department to sell more items at Tiffany cash registers. There was nothing glamorous or even admirable about it.

I was to learn later how fiercely loyal to Jackie Nancy could be. She was protective of her reputation. She was warning me away from this transactional side of Jackie's editorial career. Without saying so explicitly, perhaps without even meaning to, she was also telling me that as an outsider I'd never understand important dimensions of Jackie's style and glamor. I'd have to have experienced for decades, as she and Jackie had, the sharp-edged snobberies of the schools they'd attended and the cruelties of the society in which they circulated. Some of these amounted to blows that were crippling and could never be forgotten. Those were the psychological costs of Jackie's outward appearance and Nancy's lifelong attendance on her. They both had reason to look back on their childhoods as battlefields. Without experiencing that myself, I could only scratch the surface of her persona. It was the same as Jackie being attracted to scholarly subjects, but never being able to be a real scholar herself. I can see that now, but it was obscure to me as I started out because Nancy was just a voice on the other end of the telephone.

The second thing Nancy had to say was even more important than the first. She said she'd had to sacrifice some of her own life to be Jackie's friend.

This she said more elliptically. It doesn't surprise me from this distance that it took me a while to figure it out. I knew, for example, there was a disaster at Jackie's first publishing job. Viking brought out a novel about the assassination of a Ted Kennedy figure. Adverse publicity compelled Jackie to resign. At this point she managed to switch to Doubleday, where Nancy was already working as an assistant to the owner, Nelson Doubleday, Jr. When John Sargent, the company's chief executive officer, asked Jackie why she wanted to come to Doubleday, she replied "Because Nancy's having such fun there."

Nancy's fun came to an end when Jackie arrived. She had to give up her independence and her friendship with Nelson Doubleday, whom she liked, but whom Jackie loathed. Nancy moved to offices that were either near to, or next door to where Jackie was working. When Nelson Doubleday turned up on Jackie's first day at work and promised to find art for her cubicle, Jackie said coldly and to his face "I don't want any art." Nancy had to smooth down Nelson Doubleday's hurt feelings. She had to act as a shuttle diplomat between him and Jackie. She was now to serve as Jackie's gatekeeper at the publisher, her eyes and her ears so that what had happened at Viking wouldn't happen again. Nancy had already been doing that job for years privately, but there was now to be no escape from it. "We'd wanted to remain separate," Nancy said to me on the phone. What she meant was "I wish I could have stayed separate from her for more of my career." Almost all the stories Nancy later told me about Jackie revealed some level of practical cluelessness about everyday life on Jackie's part that Nancy had to repair. It might have been Jackie's not knowing how to use the cafeteria, or that she had to pay for her lunch, or where the trays went for the dishwashers, or who was in and who was out in the upper management of the company. All this came from Nancy knowing more about what was going on at Doubleday than Jackie did. It didn't mean Nancy was any less assertive that Jackie should appear well in my book, but it also meant, and I didn't at first hear, that Nancy would have liked to be on her own for some of the day, that Doubleday was the last chance she'd have at that, and she lost that chance. All that came to me later. As Nancy talked to me, I paced the kitchen floor and jotted notes on a piece of paper. A little clueless myself, I wondered how I'd ever persuade someone my mother's age to go deeper, to stop speaking at a superficial level, to tell me the truth.

***

The Red Lion is everyone's idea of a quaint New England inn. It's on the main street of Stockbridge, Massachusetts, a small town so perfect that it might have been dreamed up by a Hollywood props department. There's a library, a church, and small dry goods stores. The inn has a wide wooden front porch with rocking chairs. When he was alive, Norman Rockwell had a studio nearby. His *Saturday Evening Post* vision of rural American life in about 1950 seems to have survived intact there. It's less well known that the town is mainly inhabited by people with enough money to prevent things from changing. Tennessee Williams once went there to dry out from alcoholism.

Several months after our first talks on the telephone, Nancy called to say she had a book she wanted to show me. It was a 1961 biography of Jackie. It had been published to coincide with JFK's presidential campaign. The author was a society woman whom both Jackie and Nancy knew personally. Nancy thought it might be helpful to me. She had marked several passages she thought were relevant. I understood her to be saying this was an obscure book with telling details. I proposed that instead of trusting this book to the mail we meet in person. Nancy suggested lunch at the Red Lion Inn.

I approached this meeting feeling a little jumpy. What was she going to be like in person? We'd talked by then two or three times on the telephone. She was often behind a barrier of stiffness and formality. She no longer used the "How ya doin" voice, but I wasn't entirely at ease with her. I hadn't found any way to make her laugh. I drove out from Boston, where I'd moved from Chicago in order to do research at the Kennedy Library. It was a gray weekday morning in late February 2009. There were some snowflakes in the air. The ground was frozen hard.

I parked my car and walked into the lobby of the inn. There was a smoky fire and upholstered furniture last new a very long time ago. There were swags of buff-colored curtains with fussy little balls hanging along the edges. Nancy was sitting upright on a hard sofa, her back to the window. She was holding *The*

New York Times in front of her. She had on brown corduroy trousers, a brown sweater, with a single necklace, under a hand-knitted scarf around her neck, also brown. Comfy shoes. She looked a bit like a school marm, not glamorous in the slightest. She had sandy-colored hair that had peaks in it. Think whipped milk on top of a cappuccino. She wore old-fashioned glasses that looked orange to me. She was thin. My initial impression was rigidity mixed with some fragility. She was dressed to blend in, not stand out.

I approached her, shoulders rounded, and bending over. "Mrs. Tuckerman?" That was my first mistake. I thought she wasn't married, but I wasn't sure and didn't want to presume. I guessed that someone of her generation would prefer "Mrs." to "Ms." or "Miss."

She put the paper down with a crash. "*Nan-cy.*" This was a rebuke. We're all more informal now, she was saying to me, don't treat me using historic manners. I'm quite up to date, thank you very much.

I took the hand she offered, a dry, birdlike hand. Then she stood up, folded the paper, and said the dining room was closed. They only served lunch in the bar during the winter. She had a special table in mind. She wanted us to sit down at five minutes past twelve because they wouldn't hold that table. It was in a nook, separated from the other tables. She said we wouldn't be overheard there. When I was a kid, I liked reading a cartoon about spies in *Mad Magazine*. "Spy vs. Spy" made fun of Cold War skullduggery between the superpowers. Was she really going to give me top secret information about Jackie?

The answer is no. She was testing me and seeing whether she could trust me. I was trying to look and talk and behave as if I were trustworthy. I tried to be friendly and not too eager. I do remember the book she loaned me was useless. The passages she marked for me had information about Jackie that was already well-known. Perhaps, as Jackie had once personally approved these bland passages about her early life, Nancy thought I'd be happy to re-heat them and serve them up again.

She did say one or two things that may not have been new in themselves but became new as she told them to me. We were there to talk about Jackie in publishing, but she spoke of life with Jackie more generally. She remembered the helicopters coming and going at the White House after the assassination. John Kennedy kept leaping up and crying out "Daddy's home!" He was too young to understand what had happened. I'd maybe read this somewhere before, but hearing it from her, who was an eyewitness, gave the story a new poignance. In the years that I knew her, she seldom spoke of Jackie's son John. This time was an exception. She said it was a mercy that Jackie had died before him. "She loved him so."

She made clear right away that her tastes were different from Jackie's. This included people as well as clothes. Nancy remembered Diana Vreeland, the former *Vogue* editor, as being "very affected," with a strange walk and an exaggerated way of speaking. She pushed out her lips as she talked. Jackie knew that

Nancy didn't like Vreeland. She liked to tease Nancy about it. Jackie remarked how marvelous it was that Vreeland always wore black. She could save money that way. Nancy knew that Jackie was pulling her leg. If I'd been listening more carefully, I might have noticed right away how much Nancy disliked being on the sharp end of even a harmless tease.

Nancy recalled that at Doubleday Jackie was treated as a normal person after the first week or so. She enjoyed that anonymity and being thought of as nothing special. Sometimes her authors got the wrong idea and invited Jackie out to dinner. Nancy had to be the one who let them down gently. "She didn't want that." Nancy gave them phone calls to discourage them.

At one point the ice in my iced tea formed an iceberg. It caused the drink to spill out over my shirtfront as I tried to take a sip. Nancy pretended not to notice. Her greatest animation came after lunch. After he cleared away our plates, Nancy asked the waiter for coffee. He was young. He suggested he pour hot coffee on top of the cold she'd been nursing all through the time we'd been together. "Shall I pour it in there?" he asked, pointing to her old cup. "Imagine!" she whispered to me when he left. "His wanting to pour the coffee in my used cup from before lunch!" It was less a starchy disapproval of his performance than it was making some conspiratorial fun out of a trivial incident. She had a genuine love of the young and liked finding scandal in what she would have admitted was really a small mistake.

We compared notes about schools. She said the

other girls at Miss Porter's had admired Jackie for two things, her wit and her intelligence. I told her I'd been to public schools in Columbus, Ohio. I'd only been to an all-boys school for a year in London. There boys from a rival school had once cornered me in an alley. They tried to rough me up and successfully threw my shoe under a passing van. I was okay, but the shoe was so flattened I could barely wear it. She loved this. She clapped her hands. It was our most natural and relaxed moment all afternoon. Our lunch ended after an hour so. I wasn't very much wiser about Jackie's books, but I was intrigued that this woman in a plain brown sweater should have been one of Jackie's oldest friends. Opposites may attract, but I hadn't been prepared for quite this opposite. Nancy gave me the sense of a dignified, if also an anxious and somewhat brittle woman. That she should have been Jackie's longtime companion, well, that was news. She insisted, as she did every time but one for the next ten years we met, that we split the bill right down the center.

***

Western Massachusetts and western Connecticut aren't really typical of rural America. They're more prosperous and have more cultural attractions because they're really rural extensions of Boston and New York. Many city dwellers have second houses there. There are theatres, dance performances, and concerts for people who come in the summer. There's skiing nearby in the winter.

There are boarding schools and small colleges. Nancy chose to live year-round in western Connecticut after she left New York following Jackie's death. For a series of summers I too rented different houses not far from where she lived. Williamstown, Massachusetts was near us both. It's a small college town with white clapboard houses and two major art museums. We'd talked on the phone throughout 2009. I asked her questions about whether she remembered some of the people I was interviewing for the book. I told her I wanted to go to a small exhibition at the Williams College Art Museum. Maybe she'd join me and we could go for lunch afterwards?

She accepted right away. She was friendlier than when we met during the winter in Stockbridge. "There you are!" she said when she came into the lobby of the Williams Inn. It was now a hot summer day. We shuttled over to the college in my car with the air conditioning on high. When we arrived at the gallery, though, I found I'd made one of the same mistakes with her that I'd also made the first time. I thought she'd be like Jackie. She'd have the same interest in an American post-Impressionist Maurice Prendergast and his views of Paris that Jackie would have had. Instead, she walked around the exhibition quickly and was finished in fifteen minutes. I found her wandering in the permanent collection looking, bemused, at an Andy Warhol portrait of Jackie. I appeared at her shoulder. I expected her to say something about Warhol's Jackie. Instead, she just looked at me blankly, almost helplessly, and said nothing. I proposed that we go to the Clark Institute, not to see the art, but because they had a café there. She seemed relieved to be led away from Prendergast and Warhol.

When we sat down for lunch, she was happy to talk about what she remembered. She recalled Jackie flying out to Los Angeles to meet Michael Jackson. The first draft of his book wasn't long enough or serious enough. Jackie had to ask him for another draft. She anticipated meeting Michael Jackson's mother in California. Jackie asked Nancy what to take Mrs. Jackson as a gift. Nancy wasn't sure except that what Jackie proposed taking, a box of chocolates, was wrong. I asked her what she meant. She said taking a box of chocolates to a Black family was inappropriate. Why, I wondered? Because they're the same color? Her comment seemed absurd. I wasn't sure I understood. I didn't challenge her. I changed the subject.

There were other ways in which Nancy suggested the narrowness and prejudice of her upbringing. I told her that I'd met Karl Katz, the one-time head of the Jewish Museum in New York. He'd also run a film division of the Metropolitan Museum of Art. He'd once traveled to Skorpios with Jackie. Katz offered to introduce me to Jackie's longtime companion, Maurice Tempelsman. Nancy was not pleased. She warned me not to follow through with him. "I remember Karl Katz. He's pushy!" She said Jackie had dropped him. She'd take up someone enthusiastically and learn after a while the person was not to her taste. Then she'd let them go with no warning. She said Katz was one of those.

This made me feel uneasy. Two of Jackie's former colleagues, Bruce Tracy and Martha Levin, had both hinted to me separately that Nancy was anti-Semitic. Once, much later in the time we knew each other, Nancy showed me a childhood picture of herself. I said she was a good-looking little girl. "No I wasn't," she said. "I look Jewish." Another time when we were in a car driving somewhere at night she said "I didn't know any Catholics growing up." But Jackie was Catholic, I pointed out. "She wasn't very Catholic," Nancy replied.

All this was chilling. I didn't know what to do with it. I do have to report in her favor that if Nancy was uncomfortable around Black people, Jewish people, and Catholics, she was totally okay around gay men. She introduced me to several gay guys who were close friends of hers. She knew their partners too. When I told her that one of Jackie's former colleagues had sent me a picture of the Southern plantation where he grew up, she decided this was transparent flirtation on his part. "What fun you're having doing this book," she said innocently. Then she crossed her arms and enjoyed herself when I protested. What she was also saying was "I know you're gay too and that's fine with me."

She was elderly. She had been knocked down by a cab on the street in New York City. She'd had seizures. She had to make regular visits to a neurologist. She saw better with one eye than the other. At restaurants she always had to hold the menu close to her good eye to read what it said. She was also beginning to have accidents while driving. She'd driven over a road sign. She'd driven down a ravine. She wasn't hurt, but she couldn't get her door open. The fire department came. She rolled down her window. The fireman told her not to worry. He had a hydraulic tool called the jaws of life. He'd use it to get her out of the car. She ignored this and asked him instead "Will you hold my hand?"

She loved telling this story. Asking the handsome fireman to hold her hand was one of the punch lines. I heard it the first time that afternoon in Williamstown, but she told it to me again, with small differences. One was that when she was growing up her father had warned her to stay out of the papers. This was a typical upper-class parental injunction of the middle of the last century. Whatever you do, don't let me see your name in newsprint. The Connecticut newspaper where she lived reported on Nancy's accident in the ravine. It was in a column headlined "The Police Blotter" that covered calls on the local emergency services. Another of her story's punch lines was "how my father would have hated to see me in the Police Blotter."

She and I left the café after lunch. Somehow, we'd become a little more relaxed with each other. The day wasn't over yet. Could we go and have a cup of tea, she asked? We drove up to a Japanese pavilion above the main art museum. We bought hot tea in two paper cups. We split a chocolate chip cookie. We sat on the terrace overlooking the lake next to the Clark. It was still hot out. We listened to the cicadas. That's when she said, almost out of the blue, the

Onassis marriage was "a mistake." Jackie was still distraught in the years after JFK died. I think her actual line was "If your husband is shot next to you, it takes you a long time to recover." The brutality of her line surprised me. It was out of character for her, even though there was no doubting the evident truth of what she'd said. Nancy said Jackie was still unbalanced when she decided in 1968 to marry again.

I wasn't a very good reporter. I had permission to ask Nancy questions about Jackie's publishing life, because that's what she'd agreed to talk to me about. I let Nancy volunteer things about this other life, but I seldom asked about them explicitly. I think I ventured some mild defense of Jackie. It was 1968. Martin Luther King had been killed. Bobby Kennedy had been killed. She wanted to protect her children. Nancy rejected that immediately. "They only went to Greece in the summers. For the rest they were still in school here and Jackie stayed with them."

Nancy also wanted to talk about the unusual demands Jackie made on her. Once Nancy was going to visit friends in Greece. She planned to visit Jackie later. Long before she was scheduled to join Jackie, she received a phone call. "Can you come now, Nancy?" Jackie asked. "I'd like you to come now." There was no other explanation. Nancy made excuses to her friends about leaving early. Jackie sent a helicopter to pick her up. She arrived and found the habits of the Onassis household were hard to bear. Dinner was never before midnight. Onassis was doing a deal with Japan and he was on the phone at all hours. When Nancy complained, Jackie offered

"well, Nancy, do you want to eat with the children?"
Nancy didn't like that any better than the morning at
about eleven when she was sitting in the sun on the
deck of the *Christina*. A waiter with white gloves came
and brought her a glass of champagne. "I didn't want
that," she said.

A fire alarm bell rang inside the Japanese
pavilion while we were sitting on the terrace talking.
Within minutes two red fire engines came charging
up the driveway. Heavily uniformed firemen jumped
down with their axes and lumbered into the gift shop.
I suggested we should move, but no, she wasn't going
anywhere. She loved seeing the firemen. "This is the
high point of our day," she said, delighted. When the
firemen came out again, having found no fire, she
said "Oh they're so disappointed. What'll they say at
dinner?" She liked to exaggerate the news value of
any minor excitement in order to make me laugh.

I took her back to her car. She put on a pair of
Keds sneakers to drive home. They looked like shoes
my mother had once worn. When Nancy had her
shoes on, she got out of the car and stood up. She
hugged me goodbye. When I told her I could lead her
in my car out to the highway she'd need to take home,
she warned me "If you're too slow, I'll pass you." She
was entirely *compos mentis*. She knew how to make me
laugh long before I knew how to do that with her.
She knew what she was doing. The hug and the
memory of my mother, who'd died twenty years
before this, made me pause.

***

In those years there was a farm-to-table restaurant in Great Barrington, Massachusetts called Allium. It was near both of us. There were field flowers and small votive candles on the bar. There was lots of rough, exposed wood. My summer rental was ending. The temperatures were already coming down. I proposed our getting together one last time for dinner at Allium before I went back to Boston for the fall.

She was wearing a different brown sweater as her jacket and a necklace partly made up of amber. Oranges and corals and browns were the colors I saw her in most often, though she could appear in a pink golf shirt or a soft lavender sweater. She had on the orange glasses she always wore. Louis Auchincloss wore them too. James Dean once wore them. They must have been a fashion of the 1950s. My father had a pair he never wore in the back of a desk drawer.

The restaurant was uncrowded. There were few people sitting nearby us. Maybe that lay her worries to rest. Sometimes she was glad for it to be known that she had worked at the White House. That night she was ready to tell me what a chaos it had been in her office after the assassination. Tens of thousands of letters came in every day that had to be opened. The secret service was afraid there might be a conspiracy to kill the president's wife and children. They wanted everything inspected. People sent in family Bibles. Then two weeks later, they wrote again asking to have the family Bibles sent back. It was nearly impossible to find them. Nancy felt overwhelmed by all this and she did her best to cope.

JACKIE STORIES

Nancy had volunteers to help her, but they were sometimes more trouble than they were worth. Susan Mary Alsop was a problem. She was married to a famous, closeted, gay columnist, Joseph Alsop. She was herself descended from one of the founding fathers and a prominent Washington social figure. Someone even dubbed her the "second lady" of Camelot after Jackie. The Alsops entertained JFK at their Georgetown house on the night of his inaugural. She told Nancy that she couldn't come in much before eleven-thirty in the morning as she often dined out and had a late breakfast in bed. She didn't stay past one in the afternoon. She tried to meddle in Nancy's job. She warned Nancy not to allow women from the suburbs to address the envelopes of the replies to letters of condolence. Suburban women had the wrong sort of handwriting, said Alsop. She also didn't like the coffee Nancy served. Susan Mary Alsop was preposterous, but these memories of a powerful, snobbish woman still troubled Nancy forty-six years later.

Nancy was also unguarded when she recalled the period before Jackie died in 1994. As it became clear to Jackie that she would not survive her cancer, she and Nancy sat by one of the fireplaces at 1040 Fifth Avenue. They burned old correspondence. Jackie especially wanted her father's bitter letters about her mother destroyed. They couldn't get through them all. Jackie instructed Nancy to destroy them after she was gone, as well as anything else from her correspondence that might be "hot." Nancy would know which letters Jackie meant. When Nancy returned to her desk after Jackie's death, she found that all her files had been removed without anyone's consulting her. This dismayed her not only because she'd been maintaining the files for decades, but also because she couldn't carry out Jackie's orders. In the midst of her discovering that her files were gone, Caroline Kennedy appeared. "I hope you don't expect us to keep on paying you," Caroline said. Later on a mutual friend passed on another of Caroline's remarks about Nancy. "I don't know why my mother surrounded herself with people like that."

About this time, Caroline was considering running for the Senate seat in New York that had been vacated by Hillary Clinton. Nancy didn't think that Caroline was suited to political campaigning. "I don't see her eating corndogs at the fair, do you?" Nancy's more frequent comments about Caroline were hurt feelings about being overlooked and forgotten. There was a party to celebrate her appointment as ambassador to Japan. Nancy was not invited. When Caroline published her mother's oral history of the White House years in interviews with Arthur Schlesinger, Jr., Caroline had a form letter sent to Nancy rather than a personal announcement. I had the impression that a single telephone call or a visit would have removed most of these hurt feelings, but that neither one was forthcoming. Nancy's stories about Caroline changed with time. I have not verified any of them. What persisted through all the variations was Nancy's feeling unappreciated and forgotten.

Nancy believed that the Kennedy family regarded Jackie as a thing apart, not one of them.

Perhaps Caroline was simply more Kennedy than Bouvier. She was ready to dispense with Nancy's services as quickly as possible. It was a sad time for Nancy on several fronts. Doubleday had no use for her after Jackie was gone. Someone at the company cancelled the majority of Jackie's outstanding book contracts. Nancy went to live in Salisbury because it was near where she'd sometimes spent weekends away from the city while she was working.

There was another pattern in Nancy's stories. She believed that many people didn't like her. At different times she told me JFK's sisters at the wedding in 1953 hadn't liked her. Ted Kennedy didn't like or trust her. Susan Mary Alsop didn't like her. The social secretary Jackie got rid of in 1963 when Nancy was appointed, Tish Baldrige, didn't like her and never forgave her. On the other hand, one person at the Kennedy Library told me there was no doubt that the family ostracized Nancy after Jackie died. Whether Nancy's sense of being disliked was more imagined than real is hard to say.

Nancy could recover herself after a series of stories that threatened to make the evening feel tragic. I told her a story I'd read by William Manchester, the author of a book about JFK to which Jackie gave her wavering consent. He wrote that the whole time he knew Jackie, she was never quite sure where Middletown, Connecticut was. When he invited her to come visit him there, she asked him "Do I fly?" Nancy clapped her hands again. She recognized this as one of Jackie's teases. She'd ask a pretend-innocent question meant to befuddle the person she asked, while she sat back and waited for them to realize that she was making fun of them. She already knew the answer. The joke was always on them. Nancy knew how to do this routine too. When I told Nancy I was sometimes renting a small, studio apartment from a woman who lived off First Avenue when I went for several days' research in New York, Nancy asked her own pretend-innocent question. "And is she there too?" I was halfway into denying she was there when I saw what she was doing. She laughed at my confusion.

At the end of the evening she said I mustn't lose touch with her now as I was one of her closest friends. She didn't mean that exactly. It was part of her little-girl charm, an act that she sometimes put on. I was meant to be flattered, but also to smile at her exaggeration. I certainly heard what she said, though she also gave me a spooky reminder of Henry James's *Aspern Papers*. In that short story, a younger man is editing the work of a famous, dead poet. He makes friends with an elderly lady and her niece. This older woman possesses a secret cache of the poet's love letters. She offers the young man full access to these invaluable and heretofore unknown letters if, and only if, he will marry her niece. When he declines, the niece mortifies him by burning the poet's papers in the fire. The joke is on him.

***

Nancy often didn't remember much about Jackie's books. Some of what she did remember was inaccurate (e.g. "She didn't do novels!"). I thought I'd ask her about a period of Jackie's life for which she was one of the only remaining witnesses, Miss Porter's School. She liked talking about this. She said it was very much a family school. Jackie's sister had been there. Nancy's mother and sister had been there, her nieces too. This was how Nancy talked about class. She meant that the place was dominated when she went there by a small number of families who kept going there over generations. I once raised the topic of Isabella Stewart Gardner with her. Born a *nouveau riche* New Yorker, Gardner experienced social rejection in mid-1800s Boston after she married a local Brahmin. Nancy shook her head sadly, but she was unsurprised. She knew some of the Gardners. Though this had happened more than a hundred years ago, it was as yesterday to her. "You see. Family meant so much to them." She meant it still does.

Nancy's mother was concerned about family too. The Tuckermans had an old New England family tree with connections to the Mayflower settlers, a signer of the Declaration of Independence, and links by marriage to other presidential families. Nancy's being friends with Jackie dismayed Nancy's mother. It was okay that they'd begun to know each other at Miss Chapin's, but her mother discouraged Nancy from being friends with Jackie at Miss Porter's. Her excuse was that Jackie was a loner, a shy person, a reader in her room rather than a girl who liked going out and chatting with the other girls. Nancy's mother believed that this was one of the points of going to a boarding school. You made friends and useful connections there for later in life. What Nancy's mother didn't say, but which Nancy knew to be one of her objections to Jackie, was that Jackie's parents had gone through a high-profile divorce, involving alcoholism, adultery, and financial disaster. It had been in all the newspapers. That was a considerable social handicap in the days before the Second World War. Nancy's mother was also critical of Janet Auchincloss. She regarded Jackie's mother as socially ambitious. She wanted Nancy to steer clear of Jackie. As with Romeo and Juliet, Nancy's mother's disapproval may well have driven the two girls closer together.

Nancy told me she had a friend who was the school's current theatre director. He also helped raise funds for the school. He regularly came to Salisbury to call on her. She liked him. She liked his partner too. She suggested I give Eric Ort a call. He'd help arrange for us to visit Miss Porter's so I could see for myself what the place was like. We settled on a day in November 2009.

It's a beautiful place that looks more like a small college than a high school. The town of Farmington is a rich suburb of Hartford. A long main street runs through the campus. There are mature stands of trees with high canopies of leaves. There are big eighteenth and nineteenth-century houses on either side of the street. The main school buildings are in these houses. The trees were losing their leaves on the day we visited. The schoolgirls we saw were confident and polite. They went out of their way to say hello and to hold doors for Nancy. Unlike many of the college kids I'd taught in Wisconsin, they weren't shy. None of them tried to pass us while looking at her feet. We looked into the library, an art room, and the central building where the administrative offices were. An assistant asked us to stop by and say hello to the head of school before we left.

We went to Humphrey House, the dorm where Jackie and Nancy had spent their senior year at the school, 1946–47. It was a white federal style building built in 1800. Inside it wasn't luxurious. There were institutional carpets, plumbing pipes nakedly thrust across the ceilings, and bare white walls. On an upper floor there was a little brass plaque on a door marking the bedroom where the two of them had lived. It had Jackie's birth and death years, 1929–1994. Nancy's name had a blank space after the year she was born, 1928—. Inside the room was profoundly sad. The blinds were pulled down and there had been no attempt at decorating the walls, no posters, no framed family photos. There was only a single bed, not two. The bed was unmade. It had a Disney Little Princess bedspread roughly thrown across it. Nancy gave her permission for me to take a picture of her in the room and several other places. She didn't smile. She looked out the windows at the tree branches and falling leaves. Seeing this didn't lighten her spirits.

Nancy had different stories about why she hadn't accompanied Jackie to Vassar after they graduated from Miss Porter's. She told me she'd meant to, but she had a nervous breakdown and couldn't go. In another version of this story, she said she wasn't in the academic track at Miss Porter's so she wasn't meant to go to college afterwards. It was still unusual for women to have higher education in that era, and it wouldn't have been strange for her not to go on to college after high school. At another time she said it was expensive and her father, having paid the tuition at Miss Porter's, hadn't been willing to pay for college afterwards. All of the different versions of this story shared a sense of dark clouds that shadowed her at the end of her years at Miss Porter's.

A gossip columnist's story about Jackie and Nancy as debutantes lends some support to the breakdown story. Cholly Knickerbocker was a fictional figure with the first name spelled the way a high-caste New Yorker might say "Charlie." Authored by many different reporters over the years, the Knickerbocker column was nevertheless an authority on what was happening in Manhattan society. The column reported Nancy's having been the victim of a vicious snub in 1948. Nancy's mother was chair of a committee that helped to organize the series of dances that were a young girl's introduction to society. Nancy's mother had purposely left one girl off her lists. She didn't receive an invitation to an important dance. As her revenge, this girl's mother arranged a big party at home prior to the dance and invited Nancy. When Nancy arrived, she was told she wasn't invited to the party after all. She was shown the door. It was a public humiliation. This might've been the trigger for some sort of nervous trouble toward the end of Nancy's high school years. Louis Auchincloss wrote of New York society in Edith

Wharton's era that it had rules that were cruel, arbitrary, and ruthless. Maybe it hadn't changed that much when Jackie and Nancy were debs. One of Nancy's nieces told me that something—she wasn't sure precisely what—had produced a significant depression in Nancy after her time at Miss Porter's.

Nancy also told me that she'd been nervous as a small child. Her mother had taken her to the premier pediatrician and bestselling author of those years. Dr. Benjamin Spock analyzed her. He asked her to play with a big doll's house in his office while he observed her. He recommended that Nancy be held back a year and she repeated the fifth grade in school. She didn't resent this. She thought it was the right thing to do. She knew her mother and Spock were trying to help her.

Did Nancy have romantic feelings for Jackie when they were in high school? These passionate girl-girl friendships are sanctioned in a Miss Porter's school song. Student trysts are not uncommon in single-sex boarding schools. If Jackie went off to college without her, it would have been natural for Nancy to feel abandoned. Had that also affected whatever breakdown Nancy might've had?

All this is speculation. The only support for it is that Nancy never married. Greta Gerwig and Natalie Portman suggested some of the physical intimacy that might have been a part of the two women's friendship. They did this in wordless body language in the 2016 movie, *Jackie*, directed by Pablo Larraín. Certainly I never asked her anything about this. I don't think Nancy ever saw the movie, nor did she ever volunteer anything about it to me.

The presidential historian Carl Anthony recalled that when Hillary Clinton came to the White House, Nancy and Jackie passed a question to him. Republican critics claimed that Hillary was, despite her marriage to Bill Clinton, a lesbian. Did he think there was any truth in it? Anthony said there wasn't. It might well have been another tease. Was it one of their pretend-innocent questions meant to elicit a lecture from him while they laughed behind their hands?

When we finished looking at their old dorm room, we were going to meet Eric Ort in the administration building. The assistant re-appeared and said the head of school was on the phone, but she really did want to see us. Here Nancy became agitated. "She doesn't want to see us. I'm sure she's busy." She was looking for a way to get out of our saying hello. We'd been asked to wait in the hall outside the head's office like two bad girls. "Let's go," she said to me. She pulled my elbow. Then the door swung open. A stylish young woman came out and introduced herself. She was attractive, determined, and had faint lines under her eyes. She brought us back into her office. She was cordial to us both. In the midst of our conversation, Nancy wearily rebuked me for having said that she worked "with" Jackie. She wanted me to say "for." She reluctantly accepted it when I revised that to say that she'd been "a colleague." She later told me on the phone that she didn't feel right. She thought the head of school had looked her over and found her wanting. "She didn't like me. She didn't think I was grand or glamorous enough. They're always disappointed. They want me to be like Jackie was."

I murmured some protest, but what I wanted to say, and didn't, was "But you're Nancy Tuckerman. You have nothing to apologize for. That woman should have been afraid that you'd be disappointed with her." I didn't have the courage to say that to her then, but I still think it's true. Anyone who coped with a White House office after the assassination had to have had willpower and courage. That was followed by decades of running interference for Jackie, who daily encountered extraordinary problems because she was the world's most famous woman. Nancy had to have a mountain of resources inside of her. It was the wrong time to remind her of any of this. Our visit to Miss Porter's was bringing back unpleasant high school memories. Perhaps no matter where you go, or how much it costs, there are always adolescent hierarchies and inevitable failures to fit in. What Nancy and Jackie experienced as girls, whether the shame of a significant divorce, or a public snub to someone who already struggled with a nervous condition, bound them together as women. Those bad memories and their bond were invisible underneath the one's stylish appearance and the historic associations of the other's old New England name.

As I looked at the photographs I took of Nancy later I noticed her face was pinched and unhappy. I did certainly feel I had a more complex and difficult picture of both Jackie and Nancy after we visited the school. I was also left with more questions. Did Jackie exploit Nancy's schoolgirl devotion to her when she called her to Washington to replace Tish Baldrige in 1963? It was an uprooting of Nancy from her New York life. She was thrusting an anxious woman into the social secretary's job, which demanded a lot of people skills. Nancy was immediately put to the test by Tish herself. Tish had a big personality and was not shy. She needled Nancy by saying she'd have to dine out every night. She also warned her that part of the job was going in to interview the kitchen staff after a dinner party. Even though this had happened many years ago I could tell that recalling these conversations with Tish still caused Nancy anguish.

Was Jackie too overwhelmed by the assassination to consider that she was compelling Nancy to move back to New York only months after she'd required her to move to Washington? What about Jackie's will? She left millions in trust for her two children, in addition to two substantial pieces of real estate. The Sotheby's sale of Jackie's personal effects raised $34 million in 1996. Caroline put Jackie's Martha's Vineyard property on the market for $65 million in 2019. Was it enough to give Nancy just $250,000 as thanks for someone who'd given practically her entire lifetime? The will also suggests that Nancy be salaried to run Jackie's charitable foundation, but this foundation was never funded.

Or, is a friendship, like a marriage, impossible to judge for someone who isn't inside it and unable to see its private, inner dynamics? Only a year into our knowing one another, Nancy was willing to share some of the darker sides of their being together. Their friendship was less like a Hallmark card and more like the compromised, imperfect relationships most of us know.

Shortly after we left the head of school's office, Eric Ort appeared. He was a smiling young man with short blond hair and a high forehead. His real affection for Nancy and hers for him were immediately obvious. She hugged him. "Oh, Eric." Her dark mood fell away. We all three went out to a restaurant for lunch. She walked gaily in between us and held both our elbows. She said "How Jackie would *laugh* to see us walking all over Farmington!" Her mood was restored. The good Nancy was back.

***

There was then a period of seven or eight months when I didn't see her. I was writing a first draft and trying to meet a deadline. I was seeing fewer people she might once have known. I had less news to report. I did try writing an introduction to the book in which Nancy played a role. I thought maybe a quick character sketch of Nancy might help introduce my longer look at Jackie. A historian friend, to whom I described this introduction, cautioned me about it. He thought I'd better show it to Nancy before I published it. He reasoned she'd been an important source. Better not to surprise her with a document she'd never been allowed to see or comment upon. So I sent her the whole of this first draft. This would have been in the summer of 2010. If she had corrections, there was still time for me to make them.

Right away there were problems. I'd been out of the country for several weeks. I returned to find several messages from her on my cellphone. They kicked in as soon as the plane's wheels hit the runway. She wanted to talk to me. I called and left her a message that I was ready to do whatever was necessary to address her concerns, including omitting things she objected to, or rewriting passages. She didn't immediately reply. A few days later she left me a new message saying "Bill! I am incensed about what you've written. I had no idea I was going to be in the text. I'm calling Nan Talese." What I'd written about her was truthful and—I thought—flattering. She didn't like it one bit. The fact that she was going straight to the top, and not talking to me first, showed that she was ready to use whatever power she had. Whatever relationship she and I had established didn't matter.

Nan Talese managed to reassure Nancy. What I'd sent her was a draft only. Of course she could ask for changes. She told Nancy it would be best if she told me personally what she wanted taken out or revised. I then had a cold telephone call from Nancy. She was still angry. I repeated that I was ready to listen to her objections and make changes. We agreed to meet at the Red Lion in Stockbridge once again. She fixed the time. High noon. She wasn't joking.

She was late for lunch. That was unlike her. When she walked into the inn, she was grim. We sat down in the dining room, which was more formal than the bar. I remember old lace at the windows and on the tables. She was almost unlike the woman I'd known before. It was as if I'd written a character assassination of both her and Jackie, rather than, as I believed, a story of my encounters with her that may have been too frank, but which also indicated genuine admiration for them both.

She said she'd never spoken to anybody for a book before. I knew this was not exactly true. She'd helped Carl Anthony with at least two of his books when Jackie was still alive, and with another *As We Remember Her* immediately after Jackie died. She'd recently appeared with a neighbor at a book launch for a Kennedy-themed book. She was in touch with a former secret service agent Clint Hill when he was writing his book about Jackie. Nevertheless, she told me I'd betrayed her confidence by putting references to her in the book. I still have Nancy's copy of my draft, with her comments in the margins and a dozen yellow sticky notes on which she'd also written.

Nancy began by saying she didn't want me referring to Jackie by her first name. She wanted her to be "Mrs. Kennedy" throughout the book. No doubt Jackie herself preferred her first marriage to her second one, but she routinely went by "Mrs. Onassis" at Doubleday. To have used either one of her husband's last names to describe her own achievements in publishing would have been jarring. It would have been at odds with the politics Jackie herself embraced in bringing out so many books on the stories of independent women. I was incredulous that Nancy wanted nomenclature left over from the 1960s in my book. I talked this over with Nan Talese.

She suggested I put in an introductory note. I should give the reasons why I'd chosen to use "Jackie," even though it too erred on the side of informality and disrespect I didn't intend. Nancy herself was of two minds. She wrote this note on the cover of my rough draft: "When using my name either *Nancy* or *Ms.* Tuckerman."

She heavily edited a passage where I'd introduced her as one of the sources for the book. I'd failed to include an episode from her career. When she worked for Onassis at Olympic Airlines she was one of the prime movers behind the first New York City Marathon. She arranged Olympic's sponsorship for the event. She wrote that in with her blue pen above my line. She wanted to fade into the background, to be discreet, almost to disappear. Yet, she also wanted credit for parts of her career of which she was justifiably proud. She disliked seeing herself described as shy and unassuming. She proposed instead "somewhat reserved?" She was indignant that I'd described her glasses as orange. "They're tortoise shell!" She wanted the burning of Black Jack Bouvier's letters removed. "Let's forget the fireplace letters in a book such as yours." She tried flattering me as a way of getting me to delete the passage. "Your book is so much more scholarly."

Next to a page where I'd discussed Jackie's friends and the Kennedy sisters coming to pay their last respects before Jackie died, Nancy wrote "No friends ever came. This page is all made up." I had several reliable sources for those visits. There are press pictures of her friends approaching the doors of her building in her final days. It's possible Nancy just wasn't there. Why she wanted to slap me so hard—*This page is all made up*—mystified me. It was a considerable over-reaction. As she herself had given me details of how difficult it was to manage the press and the crowds at the hospital, I wondered whether she regretted telling me those things.

After the first several pages, her annotations grew less frequent. It's as if she'd thrown up her hands with the whole manuscript. She did read it, though. She caught a number of typographical errors. She flagged other passages that were confusing and certainly needed to be revised. She crossed out a line saying that some of the other girls at Miss Porter's made fun of her for following Jackie everywhere and for her dogged loyalty to her friend. "No they did *not*," she wrote. I had reliable sources for that too, though I understood why she disliked seeing it. She also edited out a line, based again on something she herself had hinted at, as well as on other sources, that at Miss Porter's Jackie sometimes had the upper hand in their friendship.

She also wanted this story of her high school years with Jackie taken out. Black Jack Bouvier had put his hand on the knee of a classmate who accompanied him and Jackie to lunch one day in Farmington. As he's gone down in the recollections of everyone who knew him as a rogue, Nancy's discretion and attempting to protect him seemed disproportionate. It was like trying to close the barn door after the horses had already run away.

She crossed out a bit where I had her saying she didn't like Onassis. "I did like Ari Onassis. He had a good sense of humor." I can remember the moment outside the Clark in Williamstown when she'd told me the opposite. Later on, she wanted the passage where she'd described the Onassis marriage as "a mistake" taken out. She later relented on this, but when she was reading my draft, she was clearly in a mood which might best be described as damage control, only it was to control whatever damage had been inflicted many years ago.

Another page that Nancy edited heavily was the part where I described Jackie's going to Doubleday after she left Viking. She wanted the whole passage about her regret that her job would no longer be separate from Jackie's deleted. She didn't tell me why, but I gathered it was because it showed too well how she felt about what happened.

Nancy also wanted a number of harmless stories taken out. She'd told me that she and Jackie once walked into a framing shop. This was after Nancy complained of her prints taking a long time to be framed. Jackie asked the shop's owner, who recognized her, how long it would take to frame a picture if she brought one in. He told her that he could have it ready for her that very afternoon. "Well, Nancy, see? Isn't that quick?" Nancy told me that she didn't want to say that the man had only offered the rapid turnaround because he was speaking to Jackie. In other words, it wasn't okay even for Nancy to refer to Jackie's being famous, or to point out that she'd been kowtowed to by the shop owner. Nancy wanted this omitted. Perhaps she also didn't like it because Jackie was once again teasing her. It sounds like another of Jackie's innocent questions meant to drive whomever she was talking to up a wall.

Nancy put a big red paper clip on a page which she labelled "sex gossip." This was a passage about Barbara Chase-Riboud's *Sally Hemings,* a novel that Jackie worked on at Viking. Its sympathetic treatment of Thomas Jefferson's Black, enslaved mistress, Hemings, was a first. Chase-Riboud believed that Jackie was interested in Sally Hemings's story precisely because she knew what it was for a woman to experience the rough side of presidential power. By 2010, when I was writing *Reading Jackie*, JFK's White House promiscuity was old news. Nevertheless, Nancy still wanted to protect Jackie from that. "Do you really want to put sex gossip in what I think of as a more literary book?" There was a prudishness and protectiveness in Nancy that went into high gear when she saw my proposed text. In ordinary conversation Nancy easily admitted that JFK had girlfriends and that Jackie knew all about them.

We'd been sitting at lunch for more than an hour as she went page by page through all these objections and more. I can't remember what we ate or drank. I think neither of us had much of an appetite. I agreed to take out much that she asked to have removed, though I persuaded her that some of the stories she'd told me wouldn't hurt anyone. No one would believe me if I painted a picture of Jackie that was as flawless as what she wanted.

By the time we were nearing the end of the draft, Nancy chose to tell me a story she'd never told me before. I left it out of *Reading Jackie*, as she asked me to. She said she liked Arthur Schlesinger, Jr., the Harvard historian who was special assistant to JFK. Schlesinger had taken the trouble to be nice to her even though the men in JFK's inner circle were mainly too busy to pay attention to what went on in her office. In the East Room Bobby Kennedy had asked Nancy to go up and look at JFK in the open casket, because he didn't want to look himself. They were trying to decide whether the casket should remain open or be closed for public viewing. Schlesinger agreed to walk up to the casket and look with her. She was grateful for his support. The president looked waxen, his head too obviously reconstructed, abnormal. They decided the casket should be closed.

At last she said she wanted the whole of our visit to Miss Porter's taken out. This was where she found I'd described her as small. "I am 5'5". I am not small!" I remember challenging her on that. "Well Nancy I'm 6'1". To me 5'5" is small." We laughed in unison and we both relented a little. Her displeasure was temporarily forgotten. She even said I could leave in some of the passage about Miss Porter's as long as I made it less snobbish sounding. I still had the feeling of being upbraided. She'd treated me as if I were a tabloid journalist. Then, when we stood up, she surprised me again. She impulsively leaned over and kissed me on the cheek. I wasn't entirely forgiven, but she also wanted me to know that she didn't altogether hate me. Later I accompanied her to her car in the parking lot. At the car door she said "You know, this was hard for me. Coming here was difficult." I appreciated that it was.

She wasn't finished with me, though. We met again for dinner at Allium in Great Barrington a few weeks later. She wanted to go over my draft again and see whether there were more things she wanted taken out. We sat down at seven and talked until nine forty-five. We both had two drinks. She wanted to hear what Nan Talese had said about my draft. She was somewhat mollified by the suggestion of an "Author's Note" that explained why I was calling her "Jackie." This led to Nancy's trying to explain why Jackie had kept her distance from Nan. She knew that Gay Talese and Nan "partied night after night at Elaine's." She knew about Gay's book on adultery *Thy Neighbor's Wife* for which he'd done personal research. Jackie wanted to avoid them, but Nancy's avidity for gossip about Nan suggests that both she and Jackie were deeply interested in Nan too. There had once been an incident where Nan had asked Nancy for the name of the woman who did Jackie's laundry. When Nancy told Jackie what Nan wanted, her response was "Don't you dare give it to her!" Isn't that an unduly harsh response to a request for a small favor? Nancy asked about Nan and when I'd last heard from her every single time we met.

Nancy and I sat next to each other on the same side of the table so we could look at her notes on the manuscript. When she got to parts she still didn't like, she'd beat my shoulder with her hand. This time she was being friendly. She was being funny. She didn't mind touching me and I didn't mind being gently thwacked. We both ordered "medium sized plates" which, under the restaurant regime of that time, meant a bony rabbit's foot for me and two scallops for her. When it came time to pay, she'd lost her wallet. She called me the next day to say she'd found it. She wanted my address so she could send me her portion of the bill. I worried about her driving home after the drinks, but she did make it home okay. I made a mental note that we shouldn't be eating and drinking after dark. We agreed the dinner portion of the evening was a joke, but we'd both enjoyed the rest. We were, a little uneasily, friends again.

***

The book was published in December of 2010, five or six months after that difficult lunch at the Red Lion followed by the dinner in Great Barrington. We were in touch occasionally, but as the book was now finished, I was seldom calling her to confirm a detail or ask whether she remembered an author. Still, I was living not too far away from her during the summer of 2011. We made plans to have dinner at one of Salisbury's restaurants in July.

I can't remember whether she still had her car then or not. After a series of small accidents, her niece had taken away her car keys. She understood the reason why it was better for her own safety, and for the safety of others, not to drive. She also resented the loss of mobility and independence. After it happened she faced up to it and was determined not to mourn for her driving days. Even friends who lived at a distance found that she managed almost as well as before by recruiting drivers. She paid them to take her around town and the countryside. There was bravery in her and it didn't die as she got older. It got stronger. I believe she asked me to come pick her up before dinner.

She gave me the address. That in itself was an advance. Before this she'd given me the street address, so I could mail things to her. She always left off the exact number of her unit. I suppose years of experience with Jackie stalkers made her cautious. I drove over to a well-landscaped complex of condominiums called the Lion's Head on the eastern edge of Salisbury. They're on a green hillside, two and three-bedroom townhouses, built in the mid-1980s. They're attractive, but also ordinary, conceived by a developer, not an architect. You could find something similar outside two-thirds of the towns in America.

Inside, however, her place felt like Park Avenue. The big living room had two different seating groups. There were two rectangular sofas in blue-green colors as well as two groupings of side chairs. There was a fireplace with an old portrait in the style of Sargent over the mantle. It was of her mother as a girl. She later told me that her father's sister had actually been painted by John Singer Sargent himself. There was also a tiny half-finished portrait of her father in a World War I uniform. Under one coffee table were newspapers, magazines, and a stack of White House books. On top of a different stack was another biography I'd written, *Henry & Mary Ponsonby*. I knew she was paying me a compliment by leaving it out and visible. As with the spilled iced tea, she didn't refer to it. She said much by not saying.

On one wall was a 1960s artist's sketch for the redecoration of the Green Room at the White House, Jackie's gift to all White House staff members at Christmas 1963. There were also small Léon Bakst pictures, his designs for costumes of the *Ballets Russes*. She said these were Jackie's gift too. "Nancy," Jackie had said to her. "If you ever need any money, you can just sell these." Nancy said drily, not angrily, "She meant if you ever need any money don't come to me." Nancy had them appraised at Sotheby's after Jackie died. She found that they were copies. Nancy was like some English people I knew who take you around their house pooh-poohing attributions of their paintings to famous painters. It's their way of making you feel at home. It's also their way of putting you in your place.

Her living room had a view of a shaded lawn, and a hillside with wild grass. There was a bird feeder hanging from a tree. She remembered a bear coming to eat from the bird feeder as she was once being taken to the hospital for pneumonia. She showed me a large, eat-in kitchen and a little study where she had a photograph of President Eisenhower and President Truman standing together. It had been taken as JFK's casket on the gun carriage stopped in front of them at his funeral. They both looked gray and shocked.

In the bedroom among a mass of framed family

pictures was a small, stunning photo of Jackie. She was wearing an evening dress with something sparkly at one shoulder. Nancy said that when Jackie died, she didn't have any good photos of her. So she asked the Kennedy Library for one. They'd sent this picture to her of Jackie in a gown. She had to rely on the archives for something to remember her by.

A former religion editor at Doubleday, now an author in his own right, told me of a conversation he'd had with Nancy after Jackie died. Thomas Cahill gave a single rose to Nancy to acknowledge the loss of her friend. Nancy took the rose with impatience. "We weren't that close," Nancy told him. When I heard this story, my interpretation was that Nancy would've disliked anyone referring to her friendship with Jackie without her bringing it up first. Another interpretation is that the two women's closeness consisted in a kind of shared distance from one another, like the later stage of a marriage where there is companionship and comfort, but without many intimacies. Was that why Nancy didn't have one of Jackie's pictures when she died?

***

During the time I knew Nancy, the restaurant where we went most often was a place called Pastorale in Salisbury. It was in a low white building, on a sloping hillside, surrounded by trees, off to the side of Salisbury's main street. It had a gravel parking lot in back. The nearby countryside was idyllic and well-maintained. I seem to recall a horse farm. Meryl

Streep lived not far away. Inside there was a small dining room, a bar, and several wooden booths along the wall. Nancy went to the restaurant often enough to be considered a regular. They brought her a drink, a Jack Daniels on the rocks, in a stemmed glass, with another glass of ice and a spoon. She didn't have to order it. They knew what she liked.

She wanted to talk about an article that had been in *The New York Times* that morning. It was about the family of Robert F. Kennedy. They wanted greater recognition at the John F. Kennedy Presidential Library in Boston. They were threatening to sell RFK's papers if they didn't get what they wanted. She was unusually interested in this. It didn't surprise her. She recalled inter-family wrangling to get Rosemary Kennedy's money long before she died. "Well, I have two children in college now," was one of the excuses put forward by a Kennedy sister as her reason for making a claim on Rosemary's money. This was the office gossip from her earlier life and she didn't mind passing on stories that reflected poorly on the Kennedy family.

She ordered an appetizer of pears, salad, and prosciutto. She pushed this around her plate. She had a second drink. She didn't eat very much. She certainly wasn't tipsy, or even close to it, but she was more forthcoming than when we'd been working together on the book. She even volunteered to come to a *Reading Jackie* book event I'd been invited to give in Litchfield, a town not far away. She was carrying a small, boxy handbag with a wooden handle. She dropped it getting out of the booth. An airline-sized bottle of Jack Daniels, empty, rolled out of it. I retrieved the purse without comment and handed it to her. My feeling about the bourbon was that she was self-medicating for a condition she'd had since childhood. I never saw her in any way out of control. On our way out, we passed a table of four people who looked up at us. They looked like happy, healthy, over-eaters. "Hi Nancy," said one of them. "Oh, hi," she said vaguely. When we got to the door, she said in a stage whisper "I don't know who they are."

***

I was a little apprehensive when Nancy volunteered to come to the book talk at the library in Litchfield. I didn't have much experience with these talks. I knew that anyone could come. I didn't know what kind of questions I'd be asked. I also hadn't realized that she'd actually want to stand up with me after the talk was over. I was flattered, but also wary. I knew there were plenty of people out there who had a fascination with the assassination. I was afraid what strangers might ask her.

Nancy sometimes lived in a state of dress insecurity. She called me the night before the library talk to say that she'd been to a local club in Sharon, Connecticut. She was surprised that all the women there dressed as if they were in New York City. She said she was going to try on several outfits for Litchfield. She didn't like dressing up. She also told me she had a nephew who lived in Litchfield. The library in the town was named for one of the signers of the Declaration of Independence, Oliver Wolcott. I knew that she and her family were proud to have descended from Wolcott.

Those may've been reasons for her taking notice, but in the end, we didn't see the nephew and no further mention was made of Wolcott on the day. I can't remember what Nancy wore. We were put into a room off to the side of the main library. There were seats for about fifty. Perhaps thirty-five people came. A woman from a local bookstore sold books in the back of the room. I had a PowerPoint presentation with images from some of Jackie's books. It took about forty-five minutes to give. I could see people's attention drifting off, their eyes glazing over occasionally. I made a mental note that thirty minutes was more than enough. I also needed more jokes.

At the end, Nancy stood up and came to the front of the room. We both remained standing for questions. One woman, chewing gum, sitting in the back row, asked Nancy whether it was true that Jackie had a New Jersey accent. I think her answer was "no" without further comment. Another, in a hushed voice, asked if Jackie gave the president's things away after the assassination. If so, what did Jackie give her? Nancy at first pretended not to hear and then said "Yes, she gave me some things," and stopped there. Later, she told me it was his backgammon set.

Afterwards we went to a local restaurant. Eric Ort and his partner joined us. A friend of Nancy's from Salisbury also came along. Brenda Nielson had been a ballet dancer and also a screenwriter for a film with Dennis Hopper. Brenda sometimes sat with

Nancy's coffee circle in Salisbury. Nancy also seemed to have a small crush on her. Maybe that's just me as a gay man noticing what he decides is same-sex sexuality everywhere. If so, Brenda took no notice. She was equally friendly to everyone and I liked her. We all had a good time talking and laughing. There were five of us at the table. I think Nancy and I both felt relieved that the presentation part of the evening was over.

Driving home from Litchfield that night, Nancy wanted to talk about Tish Baldrige again. Tish had tried to claim credit for the Pablo Casals concert at the White House, a triumph that Jackie regarded as her own. That's when Jackie decided Tish had to go. To persuade her to leave Jackie told Tish the federal government wasn't paying her enough to be social secretary. Jackie arranged for JFK's father to make Tish a lucrative offer at the Merchandise Mart in Chicago, which he owned. Nevertheless, Tish was always resentful that Jackie had given her the heave-ho. She took this out on Nancy. For years afterwards, she'd say in mock sympathy to mutual acquaintances, "Poor Nancy, she has no friends. She never got married."

Jackie had once said "Nancy, promise me you'll never write a book about me." Nevertheless, Nancy did write an essay about Jackie for the Sotheby's catalogue that Caroline and John arranged to sell their mother's personal effects. Nancy also accepted an invitation from a publisher to write about White House entertaining some years after Jackie died. The editors kept asking her to include more personal information about Jackie. At that point Nancy knew she couldn't do it without breaking her promise to Jackie. She returned the advance. Tish Baldrige had no such qualms. She took up the reins Nancy had dropped and produced *In the Kennedy Style* (1998) with the chef René Verdon, as well as *A Lady First: My Life in the Kennedy White House and Some American Embassies* (2002).

What does it say about the trust between them that Jackie extracted a promise from Nancy that she would never write about her? Had control over her privacy been so violently taken from Jackie that she couldn't quite trust anyone? Even beyond the grave she wanted to make sure her oldest friend wouldn't spill the beans?

A few months later I was invited to give another book talk at a retirement community near Salisbury. Nancy volunteered to come to that too. At some level she wanted to go on the record for having helped with my book. What at the Red Lion had been resistance and anger at my mentioning her turned into a willingness to go through some of the promotion for the book. At least locally, she wanted to make these public declarations of her association with it. Geer was a retirement community in Canaan, Connecticut. Nancy was more agitated about going there than to Litchfield. She knew people who lived at Geer. She also had a cousin who lived there. She was getting to an age where she might have to go to a retirement community herself at some point. She didn't look forward to that. When we met the woman from Geer who'd invited me, I knew Nancy didn't like her, but I couldn't say why. It was like being introduced to the head of school at Miss Porter's all over again. We were put on a porch while they arranged the room for the talk. The woman from Geer kept checking back to see if we were all right. I could see that if she asked one more time, Nancy would demand to leave.

Eventually we were led upstairs to a long room with many seats. More people came than came to the library talk. When my talk was over, I felt I'd once again made the mistake of making it too long and dull. Nancy by contrast got loud laughter when she spoke of all the buttons coming off the suits of a Russian delegation in the White House laundry. The audience also loved her when she said JFK complained that the Joffrey Ballet dancers at a White House command performance were too naked. He wanted them all to wear trousers.

Then a woman, who looked like a goth or a punk rocker, not what I expected at a retirement community, sitting in the front row, asked a leading question about Black Jack Bouvier. Was it true he used to take Miss Porter's girls out to lunch? Was it true there had been funny business beneath the table? This was a story Nancy had asked me to take out of the book and I'd done as she requested. How did this woman know about that? Nancy didn't rise to it and was blithely unconcerned. Someone else asked a question about Jackie watching JFK's scalp fly off, which, luckily, Nancy couldn't or chose not to hear. Nancy's friend from Salisbury Brenda Nielson told me later she was surprised at how vivid the assassination was for the audience even though it had occurred almost fifty years earlier.

I don't remember driving Nancy home, but I do remember feeling responsible for having subjected her to these questions. The remaining *Reading Jackie* book talks were all at some distance from Salisbury. She didn't come to those. Instead, for the next five years we saw each other regularly, mostly in the summers, mostly for dinner, and mostly with Brenda. These were happy occasions, the best of our times. The memory of them eclipses the more uncomfortable moments we spent together.

***

The summer of these book talks, Nancy and Brenda came over for dinner to a place I'd rented in Monterey, Massachusetts. It was a maroon wooden house on a rocky unpaved road. The nearest popular hangout was a summer camp for teenagers on a lake. It was not exactly a rural retreat. The neighbors spent the summer cutting down with a buzz saw one beautiful tall pine after another. There were murderous thumps all morning as the trees hit the ground. I escaped to yard sales and found a woman's 1940s black hat, with net veil attached. I had a small collection of these hats packed away in Boston. I hung the hat temporarily in the hallway on the second floor. When I showed them around the house, Nancy walked straight up to the hat and asked in an innocent voice, "Do you wear this around when no one's here?"

When we sat down to dinner Nancy had a few new White House recollections. Brenda and I both knew better than to ask her to remember those days, but she sometimes volunteered if she was in a good mood. She said White House parties in the short time she was there had plenty to drink and lots of beautiful women. She once asked the White House's chief usher why the swimming pool was blocked off after lunch time. He said merely "Nancy, you ask too many questions."

In Salisbury Nancy occasionally struggled with being alone. She had a buzzer that summoned the emergency services, which she sometimes pressed by mistake. She then had to deal with urgent telephone calls demanding to know what was wrong. She could be hard on herself, especially if she caused anyone trouble, and sometimes if she didn't. She took yoga classes, perhaps because she found they helped her stretch and kept her calm. If she didn't get a pose right, she'd make herself do it over and over again until she did. She was on beta blockers for high blood pressure. They also helped with her anxiety. She could still be exacting of family members. If she didn't get a thank-you note for a Christmas gift within a reasonable time, she'd let the recipient know her disapproval. Sometimes she'd even withdraw or withhold the gift in future years. She had fun seeing her coffee circle in the mornings, a mainly male group, several of them nice guys in blue collar jobs. At least once they all dressed up to go out for a formal dinner with her and called themselves "Nancy's men."

The next summer we all met again for brunch at Pastorale. I showed up a little early and so did Nancy. We sat at an outdoor table near the Salisbury pharmacy where her coffee group met. She was wearing a floppy sun hat. A tall man, a middle-aged smoothie, dressed as if for a country club, showed up and said hello to her. She was pleased to see him and introduced me to him. After he left, she told me that his family owned several blocks around St. Patrick's Cathedral. Now that her car had been taken away, she often relied on him for a ride into town. One morning he called her and said he'd be at her house in fifteen minutes. "But" she protested, "I'm not dressed yet." "In that case," he said, "I'll be there in five." She adored that. His speaking to her as if she were under thirty rather than over eighty made her feel wonderful.

When we got to Pastorale the owners came over to say hello to her. Nancy said that one of them was also helping her by driving her around town occasionally. This woman had a two-year-old daughter who was sometimes in the car with them. She remarked within Nancy's hearing that Nancy liked the two-year-old better than Nancy liked her. Nancy pretended not to have heard. It was a small indication that she had the capacity to make life difficult for people other than me, and her silence said that she didn't want to be teased about it. Nancy went out of her way that day to be nice to me. "Oh I wish you were writing another book about Jackie so we could see each other more often." She didn't mean anything close to that. She was using a deliberate exaggeration to make me feel wanted. It was her way of addressing me as if I were under thirty.

The following year, we were again three, Nancy, Brenda, and I at dinner. I know it was April of 2013 because the Boston Marathon had just been bombed. Of the two perpetrators, Tamerlan and Dzhokhar Tsarnaev, Nancy said "I wouldn't dream of pronouncing their names." It was as if a terrorist incident could be reduced to getting the names right in conversation. You might say this was typical of a woman who'd written an updated version of the *The Amy Vanderbilt Complete Book of Etiquette*. She could only see the world from that narrow point of view, but then you'd be missing the sly way she was also making fun of herself.

Nevertheless, she could also be severe about social rules and she wasn't always playing. She did not approve of my having written a novel about the queen of England without the queen's permission. She denied that the queen's being a public figure gave me that license. I should have written to ask her. When she ordered the pears and prosciutto again, I asked if she always ordered that from the menu. She said to me "Don't point!" and changed the subject. Later she mentioned that she'd been invited to an event at the Kennedy Library. She was going to decline. I encouraged her to go. She turned to me sharply and said "I suppose you'd like to take me, wouldn't you?" Even though my book was done and I'd moved on to other projects, she could still deliver a verbal slap. She knew how to make it sting.

She told the story of going to teach very young

children about manners. This was either at a pre-school or a church. She enjoyed being with them. She later met one of these children on the sidewalk in town. "How are you?" she asked. Instead of "Fine," as she'd taught him to reply, the little boy said easily "Good." She was exasperated, when she ought to have been amused.

Nancy disliked Lee Radziwill very much. Over dinner she said Lee was a "witch." Lee had once insulted and embarrassed Nancy at a large party by saying "here comes the fastest typist in New York." That Lee should have taken the trouble to insult Nancy so publicly suggests she was a great deal more than Jackie's typist and Lee knew it. Lee's daughter Tina sometimes lived with Jackie in her apartment as a refuge from her mother. Lee called Tina one Christmas Eve from the Bahamas when Tina was staying with Jackie's family in New York for the holiday. Tina was called to the phone, spoke to her mother, then hung up, and burst into tears. When asked why, Tina said her mother had just criticized her for sounding too American. "You should never lose your English accent!" According to Nancy, Tina had to visit a psychiatrist twice a day afterwards. Nancy said more than once to me that Jackie and Lee were not close, and indeed that Lee had not come to Jackie's bedside when she was dying. This seemed a bit severe to me and I wondered whether it was true. There was some jealousy in the air when Nancy talked about other women who might have been close to Jackie. She was skeptical when I reported that Carly Simon had said Jackie was her good friend.

Our talks were not all harsh passages. There were also jokes and fun. One time she spilled a little of her drink on Brenda's blouse. "Oh Brenda!" she said "you'll have to take it off." Brenda laughed and warned her "Now, Nancy!"

***

One summer evening, Nancy, Brenda, and I met at a tavern in Sheffield, Massachusetts. The Stagecoach was a casual place, in a wooded setting, with a barn-like feel. The service was too casual for her. It took a long time for the waiter to bring our drinks. She sent me to go and find out what the problem was. When the drinks came, she was in a better mood, but she told a story that returned to one of her more troubling themes. At a dinner at the St. Regis in New York, she'd been seated next to the conservative talk show host, William F. Buckley, Jr. He made no effort to talk to her. He spent the evening talking to his partner on the other side. She was humiliated. Then she added, "Maybe I wasn't worth the effort." In some moods, she actually believed that. When she was feeling well, she would have laughed off Buckley's bad behavior as something that reflected more poorly on him than on her.

It's too easy to say her insecurity arose from having had an unfulfilled crush on her best friend from Chapin and Miss Porter's. That may have been a part of the puzzle, but my sense was that she shadowboxed with many phantom demons for much of her life. She still lacerated herself for something that had happened when she was a little girl. She told me several times of this incident. Her parents took her to visit Sara Delano, Franklin Roosevelt's mother, who was also a cousin of theirs. When they returned home, Nancy got up on the sofa, danced around, and did a little singsong. "I met the president's mother! I met the president's mother!" Her own mother reprimanded her for this. This caused her such a sense of shame that it was still bothering her in her eighties.

Someone remarked to me that in the days when Nancy used to smoke, she would hold off all day, but allow herself a drink and a cigarette after six p.m. An hour later the ashtray next to Nancy was so full that it was over-flowing. My guess is the cigarettes helped calm her down. The drink helped her be less hard on herself.

Nancy also had complex resentments of Jackie that may have been as attributable to her own shyness as to Jackie's own sometime sense of entitlement. She told a story of Jackie's maid asking her to take some of Jackie's cast-off clothes. They were in a room in Jackie's apartment at 1040 Fifth Avenue. These were cocktail dresses and evening gowns meant for an elaborate social life. Nancy's own night life was nothing like that. She had no use for the clothes. The maid replied that Nancy should take them anyway so Jackie would stop asking her about them.

What was this story about? Why couldn't Jackie just call Nancy into her bedroom and say "Nancy, do you like this dress? Do you want it? Why don't you take it?" Or was Jackie being delicate? Did she know very well that Nancy would have no occasion to wear the dresses? Was she suggesting instead that Nancy just take them to a consignment shop and sell them? Was it her way of tipping Nancy, whom she probably didn't pay very much? It's hard to know what was at work in Nancy's telling of this story, except that it seemed to indicate that there were realms of ordinary experience that the two friends found it difficult to talk about between themselves. The maid had to play go-between.

Nancy did have one comic story on the same subject. She told it at her own expense. She had a sister, Cynthia, who lived in a retirement community near Boston. Nancy drove up to visit her. At the dinner hour Nancy wore a slim pair of gray wool trousers. Her sister objected. "Nancy! You can't wear those. You have to wear a dress into the dining room." Nancy defended herself. "But Cinnie! These pants belonged to Jackie Onassis!"

Nancy could be in different moods forbidding or fearful. She could also be self-aware. She had a talent for dry, understated humor, and silly hyperbole. I usually worried in advance of meeting her about whether my manners would be up to her mark. I ended by forgetting all that and enjoying her company. I ceased to think of her longterm friendship with Jackie as anything like that of mine with my own close friends. The power differential between them may have outweighed the intimacy that came from their long-shared experience. And yet, with so many people around her she could not trust, so many who wanted something from her, Nancy must also have been a rock for Jackie.

If I was on my guard with Nancy, I always wanted to see her again. It wasn't just because she'd been a witness to history and knew better than anyone what it was like to be around Jackie. When I was sitting with her, I just found myself waiting for whatever she'd do and say next. She may have been elderly, but she still knew how to entertain. She may not have always been aiming for that, but that was the end result. Her occasional nervousness and uncertainty were versions of traits I had myself. Her living a single, unmarried life, and approaching old age without the support of a partner, well, that was my life too.

***

Then in about 2015 Nancy's life grew worse. She had a health crisis, gave up her condominium, and went to live at Geer Village. When her health crisis grew worse, she had to leave Geer, where they couldn't cope with her medical needs. She moved to Noble Horizons, a retirement community nearer where she used to live in Salisbury. She once explained to me that she didn't want to go to any retirement community. If she had to, however, she said she'd prefer Geer because the main meal there was in the evening. You could have a drink beforehand. Whereas at Noble the main meal was at lunch. It was a small distinction about mealtimes and cocktail hours. I knew what she meant.

By the time I arrived in her neighborhood that summer, she was installed at Noble, against her will, and confined there by medical orders she didn't understand. I knew from Brenda that Nancy had been in a bad way. I called her at Noble and asked if I could come see her. She suggested I come at two the next afternoon. I could hear a nurse in the background dictating instructions she wanted Nancy to repeat to me about how to find her. I also overheard the nurse telling her she couldn't leave the premises. She sounded a little confused on the telephone, perhaps a little drugged. She was enough herself, however, to do a little-girl routine. "Oh, I can't wait till you come." The old Nancy was still in there somewhere.

On the tenth of August 2015, I drove out to Noble Horizons in Salisbury. The name itself sounded as if it had been made up by some public relations person with a clumsy attempt at euphemism. The buildings themselves were not bad looking. Many of them had dark wooden exteriors. They stood in a handsome grove of trees. It might've been an upmarket summer camp. I parked and went indoors. Inside it was more depressing. The furniture had the fake bamboo and stiff polyester upholstery of a mid-range roadside motel.

Upstairs, Nancy's room was more distressing still. There was a single hospital bed with a plain brown bedspread. Next to this was a reclining chair made from plastic to resemble leather. The nurse spent the night next to her. She was never allowed to be alone. There was a small table facing the window.

She was sitting on a cane chair at this table with her back to the door. She was writing some notes in her old handwriting on blue-bordered cards. A nurse dressed in blue was bending over her. There were two black and white photos of her father in childhood on the table.

There was also a sky-blue love seat, its cushions still imprinted with the bottoms of previous visitors, and an undistinguished carpet. Linoleum covered most of the floor. A reproduction of Aaron Shikler's White House portrait of Jackie had been tacked up on the wall, unframed. I doubt Nancy herself had put it there. The nurse excused herself to go and get some coffee. The two of us were alone. She didn't wail about her fate, nor do I think she understood she was now there for the duration.

We talked of people we both knew. She hadn't seen a mutual friend from the Kennedy Library in a while. She missed him. He had been out to visit her, however. She remembered that. She was tired of having the nursing staff always in the room with her. She called them "the assistants." It made me remember that once, early on in our relationship, she'd bridled when I said she'd served as Jackie's "secretary" instead of "Jackie's assistant."

When I stood up to go after forty minutes, she was more effusive than usual. She insisted on walking me downstairs to the front door. A hospital bracelet she was wearing that must have had a sensor inside it tripped off an alarm as we left her room. Two or three nurses came running after us. Nancy turned and admonished them. "I'm just saying goodbye to him."

They stood back and gave us some distance. When we got to the front door, she said to me "I loved talking to you." She turned and allowed herself to be led away by the assistants.

The next summer, she was thinner, but in somewhat better shape. She was happier and more resigned to living at Noble Horizons. She'd been diagnosed with a lung condition. She could only walk with a walker. She had an oxygen tube under her nose and she had to carry with her a small oxygen tank. Nevertheless, she was in good spirits. She was being allowed the liberty of going out to lunch. She pretended as if we were escaping from a hated reform school.

The nurse helped us put her walker in the back of my car. "I don't need it. I can take your arm. We're taking it to please *them*." The assistants. We drove to the White Hart Inn. For most of the time I'd known her, the White Hart had been closed and up for sale. Now it had new owners. It had re-opened. On a weekday they served lunch in their tap room. We came in the front door and walked through the lobby. The man at the front desk recognized her and called out to welcome her. She waved at him. Then we went into the wood-paneled bar. A waitress and the bartender both said hello and treated her as if she were a special guest. We sat down at a corner table with padded benches. We ordered two glasses of white wine and two cups of celery soup. For dessert we split a plum crumble with a scoop of ice cream.

She loved hearing a story about Greg Lawrence so much that I told it to her again. He'd collaborated with his wife the ballerina Gelsey Kirkland on several different books for Jackie. After Jackie died, he'd wanted to write a book about Jackie in publishing. Doubleday turned him down. Then when Doubleday commissioned my book instead, he'd managed to sell his book to a rival publisher. When a *New York Times* reporter asked Lawrence what Jackie would have thought of me, he replied "Jackie wouldn't have let William Kuhn do her laundry!" Nancy almost wept. She laughed that hard. She wanted me to tell it again. The sequel to this story was that Nan Talese called me and told me not to reply to Lawrence if *The New York Times* asked for a rejoinder. She thought it would give his comment more attention than it deserved. Nancy calmed down then. She stopped laughing. She said one of her first approving things about Nan Talese. "She was correct."

She asked whether I'd heard from our mutual friends. I couldn't raise them on my cellphone so we taped a little cellphone video for two of them. I suggested how a man I knew who ran a Jackie fan page on Facebook, would like it if we recorded something for him too. She didn't know him, but she agreed at once. When I introduced her using her name on the video, she added in a very small voice, "I'm a very famous person." She was being funny in a low-key way only she knew how to do.

The very first time I met Nancy at the Red Lion Inn I expected a great lady, self-assured, *soigné*, confident of her position in the world, someone who'd worked at the White House, sailed on Onassis's yacht, and been at Jackie's side for most of her life. Though she'd done those things, Nancy was never that. She always stood erect and sat up straight, but she was more vulnerable than that posture suggested. She was susceptible to her own criticisms of herself and to criticisms she imagined others had of her. She was a more touching woman than I expected. She's under my skin even now.

At the White Hart for the first time she wanted to pay the bill. She handed me some notes from her pocketbook and asked me to leave the tip. She left it to me to decide on the amount. "I want to be generous," was her only instruction. It seemed like her *envoi*.

When we got her walker and her oxygen canister back to Noble Horizons, we found a nurse waiting for her at the entrance. I helped her out of her side of the car. "Let's not say b-y-e," she said looking me in the eyes and spelling out the word. "We've had a wonderful time together." She gave me a warm hug. Then she turned to the nurse and walked a few steps in her direction. Nancy wanted to know why the nurse hadn't brought a wheelchair. "I have to walk all that way?" she asked, a little querulously.

We had one or two more telephone conversations before she died in the summer of 2018 at age eighty-nine. I called her after the election of Trump and asked her what she thought. "Well, he has all that money so he must know what he's doing." It wasn't actually an endorsement, but it was a conventional, depressing response from a woman who'd worked in the White House during one of the most eloquent and most idealistic presidencies in modern history. I oughtn't to have looked to her for originality or comfort at that moment. I had to remind myself that both she and Jackie had grown up in conservative, Republican households. It was only Jackie's marriage that brought them into Democratic politics. By today's standards, JFK wasn't that progressive, nor do historians think of his short presidency as very productive. What Nancy gave me was something much more important than political insight.

She taught me it was possible to come from a fortunate background and still to be burdened with a nervous temperament, a real disability even though what she feared sometimes wasn't there. In Nancy's telling Jackie became a somewhat more shadowed but also a more three-dimensional presence than she was in my mind beforehand. There were passing cruelties and teases between them that Nancy had not forgotten. Nevertheless the warmth of their friendship must be measured by the many years the two women chose to spend together. If Jackie became more flawed, more manipulative, and less generous in Nancy's telling, it's Nancy herself I'll always remember, because it was her demanding and affectionate presence I learned to know in person. Jackie probably took advantage of Nancy's selfless devotion to her. She was the stronger of the two, and their relationship has distinct parallels to JFK's with Lem Billings. Like Jackie and Nancy, Jack and Lem were friends since boarding school. Like Nancy, Lem never married. It can be said of Nancy's attachment to Jackie, as it was also said of Lem Billings and JFK, that Jack Kennedy was Lem's *raison d'être*.

If Jackie was attracted to, but never quite understood the world of scholarship, I don't think I've ever entirely grasped what it was to live among shipping tycoons, Mayflower families, and urban socialites. I do now dimly understand that it is impossible to know the secret of Jackie's mystique without also acknowledging the woman she kept by her side for so many years. Nancy wasn't always unsure of herself, but she did give the impression of a glass that could easily shatter. That Jackie should have chosen to stick by Nancy was a token not only of love and loyalty, but also of dark days they'd been through together as teenagers. Even when she was within weeks of dying of cancer, Jackie wanted help to destroy evidence of her parents' hostility toward each other. She found that only with Nancy. It wasn't records of the assassination that troubled her at the end, but records of her parents' divorce. That was what bothered her most within sight of her own grave.

Similarly, Jackie was Nancy's best friend at a time when humiliation at a debutante party sent her into a tailspin. The flipside of Jackie's glamor was childhood shame and clinging to a friend who had long-lasting psychological stress of her own. If all of us try hard to present our most pleasing and our most attractive faces to the world, to conceal what continues to bother us long after the event, may we also have such dedicated friends to stand by us. One of Nancy's friends told me after Nancy died that she saw her as a heroic woman who forfeited her own life to help and to advise her famous friend. My own dominant memory of Nancy is a little different. I still remember her telling another story at her own expense. It was of her mock desperation in her car, in the ravine, with the fireman. She liked telling it again. She'd re-arrange the punch lines to extract the maximum fun from it. Above everything else, Nancy loved to laugh.

2 A Rival at Work

If knowing Nancy Tuckerman reveals something new about Jackie, then there's also insight to be had when we look at a woman who, even comparatively briefly, Jackie regarded as a rival. Jackie and Nan Talese had a lot in common. They were about the same age. They both worked as women in a publishing world dominated by men. The two women overlapped as editors at Doubleday for about five years. Nan arrived in 1990 after a distinguished and much longer career begun at other publishers. Jackie had been there since 1978. They were from similar backgrounds. They both went to private schools. They both grew up as Catholics and debutantes in and around New York City. They both married prominent men. Their husbands humiliated them both in high-profile adulteries.

Nan was one of the best-known editors in the country and had a more substantial list than Jackie did. She also had more contacts in the industry as she'd been working in publishing since 1959. Jackie didn't come to editing until 1975, after her second husband died and her children were grown. Nevertheless, both women were readers. Both women dressed stylishly. There was good reason for them to be allies and friends. Instead, there was a quiet wariness between them, which occasionally became coldness and a tendency to avoid one another. A brief look at their rivalry makes it clear that Jackie's later life wasn't always as easy as you might imagine. She had to cope with her own office politics. She sometimes made mistakes. She sometimes retreated behind the force field of her celebrity when she might have grown and learned something new.

Because she had less experience Jackie had reason to feel a little less secure than Nan did. She didn't like being reminded of it. Nan once told me of what she regarded as a *faux pas* on her part. All the editors at Doubleday had been asked to fill out a form in which they accounted for their time during the day. Jackie brought her form into Nan's office and asked her how to fill it out. They discussed it a little and then Nan remarked, "But, of course, you're only part-time." This was true. Jackie was in the office three or four mornings a week and often left after lunch time. She was away during the summers. She worked from home and often met her authors for working sessions in her apartment, but she did not have the kind of everyday, or hourly presence in the office that Nan and the other editors did. Jackie didn't like Nan's saying this out loud. Nan noticed that as soon as she said it, Jackie's expression changed. It was as if an iron gate clanged down in a castle. Their conversation was at an end. Jackie turned and left Nan's office.

Jackie had a chance most editors didn't have. She was allowed to dabble, to experiment, to try out a new career after the age of forty. She was allowed to choose projects to work on almost, though not entirely, independent of whether they'd sell well or not. She was able to mix genres, including children's books as well as books for adults, large format illustrated books for the Metropolitan Museum of Art as well as expansions of articles she'd liked in *People Magazine*. This was unusual among working editors then. Her wide remit was a privilege that came to her because of her fame. The fact of Nan's referring to it, the fact of Nan's having a distinctive and literary list that she'd acquired through more work than Jackie had ever done in the publishing trenches, suggests several new possibilities about Jackie's character. She could be jealous of her colleagues. She wasn't always easy to deal with. She was more likely to be impatient with someone from her own social background than from someone beyond it. Her rarefied upbringing—and Nan sometimes suffered from this too—could be a disability as well as an asset.

Now in her eighties, Nan retired at the end of 2020. During her career she edited many of the best-known writers of her generation, including Margaret Atwood, Robert Penn Warren, Antonia Fraser, George Plimpton, and Ian McEwan. She's probably the only living editor who's ever crossed swords on television with Oprah Winfrey. She began as a copy editor at Random House and rose to be the first female literary editor there. She acquired fiction that later became legendary, including Thomas

Kenneally's *Schindler's List* when she was at Simon &
Schuster, and Atwood's *The Handmaid's Tale* at
Houghton Mifflin. Along the way she married the
writer Gay Talese, who published his own landmark
books, as well as classics of literary nonfiction in
Esquire magazine. Nan has attributed her survival to
sticking to the editing side of the business and never
aiming for management. There's a great deal more to
her longevity than that modest disclaimer would
suggest. What were formerly more than a dozen
independent publishing houses have contracted and
consolidated into five, which may soon be four. The
advent of Amazon and ebooks have turned
publishing upside down, yet she continued to acquire
and edit well-known books throughout this period of
upheaval.

I talked to Nan on the phone for the first time in
the summer of 2008 soon after she acquired my book,
Reading Jackie. My British agent said that it was
appropriate for Nan to edit a book on someone
informally regarded as an American queen because
Nan herself was queen of the New York publishing
scene. I must treat her accordingly. My American
agent also chimed in before introducing her to me via
a three-way telephone conversation. He coached me
about what to say. He told me to keep the
conversation light. I know I felt intimidated, but there
was no need. On the phone she was laughing and
cheerful. It was almost like talking to a family member
who approved of me in advance. What I might have
also realized, though I only see it now, is that queens
are expert at reducing the distance between you and

them. They do it in half a dozen words, with a bantering sense of mutual respect, and an almost comic assertion of equality between you.

The first time I met Nan in person was in New York. The publisher's offices were in a tall building indistinguishable from half a dozen others nearby. I went up in the elevator. One of her assistants brought me from the reception area back to her office. Nan was on the phone. I sat on a sofa in the hall outside her office door to wait for her. I could overhear her bright voice speaking on the telephone. I guessed she was talking to an agent who was asking why Nan wasn't interested in a book project she'd sent her. "Not my cup of tea!" said Nan with a lighthearted giggle. Then she came out in the hall to introduce herself to me. She was then in her seventies, but she looked two decades younger than that. She was wearing a string of pearls that came down to her waist. There was a kind of whimsical extravagance about her. She might've been a 1920s flapper. She was friendly. She was bubbly and surprisingly honest. She was also formal. She spoke in the Anglo-American accent that you sometimes hear spoken in Hollywood films of the 1940s and '50s. She was definitely my cup of tea.

She took me out to lunch. We went to Petrossian, a restaurant known for smoked salmon and caviar. I'd once seen their smoked salmon mentioned as an essential ingredient in a recipe. I thought to myself as I stood in my grad student kitchen in Baltimore, how will I ever get that? How will I ever get there? It seemed impossible. Yet, there I was at lunch with Nan

Talese. I wasn't even paying the bill. Reader, sometimes in life what happens to you is even better than what you allow yourself to dream. It felt very near to what it might've been like to sit down with Jackie herself.

Nan told me stories of how she'd started in publishing. She remembered being a junior editor. Her office was in the basement. She dared to write a marginal comment on a manuscript of Robert Penn Warren's. She thought one of his characters needed more introduction. She cringed when Warren wrote back "I think you'll find that character was introduced as early as page fifteen."

She spoke of her marriage. She and Gay were in bed together early in the morning. They were both young. She didn't want to wake him because she wanted him fresh for his writing day, though she had a job of her own and needed to go to the office. She also said that he was now writing a memoir. He was going to discuss their marriage. She didn't want it discussed in public. She wondered whether she ought to sue him. She'd consulted the lawyers at Doubleday about how to prevent him from quoting her letters. She said this dispassionately, without bitterness or anger. She loved him. She had no intention of divorcing him or ceasing to live with him. So much truth-telling in a person I'd just met semi-shocked me, but it also won me over to her side.

The second time I met her she was wearing a blue, knit jumpsuit. I took one glance and said silently to myself, I want to look that good when I'm seventy-five. We discussed Caroline Kennedy's having asked me not to quote from her mother's letters. Nan told me she hated quotes in manuscripts anyway. She just wanted the news. Without making too much of it, she was lightly teaching me the difference between academic writing and writing for a broad audience. Among academic historians a direct quote indented from the rest of the text is prized. It's usually from a historical source found by traveling to a distant archive or discovered among a trove of unexamined papers. It's a mark of a scholarly manuscript's value and authenticity. When you're not writing for historians, the story is the thing. You shouldn't burden the reader with quotation marks unless it's something brief and spectacular. She had a crisper idea in her mind than Jackie did of how scholarship was different from the books she wanted to produce and me to write. Nan's books might eventually achieve some status as literature or history. She left all that to the chance of criticism and passing opinion. In the short term she wanted few quotes and a gripping narrative.

I was still wearing my historian's hat. I remember telling her at that same meeting about an archival discovery I'd made. It was in Diana Vreeland's papers at the New York Public Library. Vreeland had once asked for a letter of introduction from Jackie. They were working on Vreeland's book *Allure*. Vreeland's fame was almost as great as Jackie's. Why would she need a letter of introduction? It seemed silly to me. Nan didn't think it was funny. She asked me if I wanted one of those letters from her too. She was wide-eyed and wanted to be helpful. She was used to the outsized insecurities of writers. If it would help me produce the book on time, she wanted to give it to me, right away, no questions asked. I thanked her and said I thought I was okay without it. I didn't say to her that the fact she was editing it meant that I needed no further introduction. I was too embarrassed to point out what seemed to me obvious. Like Nancy Tuckerman, I thought it would be better not to point out Nan's own legend to her while I was sitting with her in her office.

We remained on good terms during our time together, even when Greg Lawrence proposed to write his book on the same topic as mine. He wanted his book out first. Nan was alarmed. She called me on a Sunday morning in Boston and wanted to know everything I knew about Lawrence. Doubleday had spent money on my book. She thought his book would injure our sales. She sent out a letter to a list of contacts I gave her saying my book would be authoritative, while his would be salacious. She backed me in moving forward with our book as quickly as possible. This required her to speed up the publishing machinery that often requires up to a year between delivery of a manuscript and actual publication. We beat him. Nan still read every chapter and made suggestions at every stage. She wasn't just an editor who commissioned a book and then left it to others when the manuscript was delivered. She actually edited. I still have a draft with her notes in blue ink down the left-hand margin. Nor were all her comments compliments. On the first draft of one chapter I could sense her increasing exasperation in the marginal remarks. I felt like a student who has dared to annoy the professor. I liked being read by her, being told in effect, re-do this please. She'd noticed me. She'd spent time on my work and that was flattering enough. Jackie was certainly an active and intervening editor toward the end of her editorial career, but not at first. Gathering that confidence took some time. Whereas Nan, down in her basement office, had already dared to challenge a well-known writer long before Jackie had even come on the scene. I was the beneficiary of that.

Jackie slowly built up a list of unusual books as an editor, some of them unusually successful. Bill Moyers's books, based on his interviews with prominent figures on public television, all sold strongly. Jackie also brought out Larry Gonick's zany *Cartoon History of the Universe*, which was a hit before graphic novels became popular. Jackie's signing up a novel by Dorothy West, the last significant figure in the Harlem Renaissance, was not only successful, but also of literary importance. If Nan's choices were a byword for merit even before they were reviewed, Jackie showed that she was more than a celebrity hire who was only good for her public relations value to the company. She cultivated her own taste for what interested her in a book. Her list was idiosyncratic and unpredictable. There was high culture in her books on photography and ballet, but there were also books related to her personal connections. She knew both Bill Moyers and Dorothy West personally. Bringing up children gave her a feel for what might be appealing in a comic book popular history.

Jackie and Nan may have spoken little, but they both kept tabs on what the other one was doing. Once when Nan was bringing out a big coffee table book on women's hats, the higher-ups at Doubleday allowed her the luxury of incorporating a costly red grosgrain ribbon in the book's cover design. When Jackie discovered this, she hissed to the designer "How'd she get to do that?"

I omitted some of the details of this from my book because I didn't want to embarrass Nan. I suspect Nan already knew. When it came time to design the cover for my book, she made a point of incorporating a red ribbon as a design element in the cover for *Reading Jackie.*

Tom Cahill sat for a time in an editorial office adjacent to Jackie's. He showed her his proposal for a series of linked historical volumes he was going to write for Nan. He called it *The Hinges of History* with *How the Irish Saved Civilization* as its first part. Jackie was angry. She wanted to know why he hadn't given it to her. Cahill believed that Jackie in her own mind towered above Nan. There was a quiet arrogance under Jackie's unflustered surface. This only showed when she missed out on something she believed ought to have been hers.

At one point I went to meet Nan at her house. We were going over Jackie's Doubleday sales figures. This was a subject of secrecy. Nan made clear that I could not publish any of the sales figures for Jackie's books. Doubleday considered this proprietary information and didn't want it public. I pressed a little on this. How could it possibly matter now? The last of Jackie's books had been published ten years ago. How could that be giving away anything important? Putting some of the figures in my text could help distinguish her good bets from her bad ones. Nan was firm on this and she didn't want to talk about it. She would allow me to discuss books that were in a top-selling category, those that were medium, and those that had not performed so well. This sensitivity to publishing actual sales figures seems excessive even today. I accepted Nan's verdict, even though I knew it was contrary to what readers would want to know. She had on her inside-publishing blinkers and I knew that I couldn't remove them. Each woman had her blind spots.

I confined myself to looking around her house. It was an old brownstone on the Upper East Side. It had the feeling of having been decorated professionally in the 1970s. There was shiny foil wallpaper in an interior dining room. There were some clouded mirrors as the backdrops to nonworking fireplaces in the living room and study. The ceilings were high and stately. It was a little dark. It was decorated with her daughter's oil paintings of industrial landscapes. While we sat together on a sofa, a dog walker brought in a pair of black, barking, Scottish terriers.

Nan often looked perfect and her attitude to me was always friendly, but I knew she was putting a brave face on what was sometimes a difficult job. She mistakenly copied me on an email to her daughter when there were difficulties about the cover of the book. There were disagreements about color, design, and the use of an expensive photograph. The tone in the message was mild despair. She was having difficulty staying calm after going through a protracted design process. A lot was riding on the publication of my book. There was an advance that had to be recouped. She was feeling the stress. She never showed that to me, though she confessed it to her daughter. Nan was practiced at putting on a calm and untroubled face when there was much to be worried about under the surface. That was something she and Jackie had in common. They both had a cool imperturbability that may have been a by-product of their don't-rattle-the-teacups upbringing.

Nan told me a story that indicated she sometimes might have had either a tin ear or possibly even some aggression in her attitude to Jackie. The British novelist D. M. Thomas received worldwide acclaim for his 1981 novel *The White Hotel.* He afterwards wrote a new novel that Nan wanted to publish. The problem was that it had a dream sequence in which the narrator descended a staircase to find JFK's open casket. Nan asked the president of Doubleday whether she could publish it. He advised against it. Nan then asked Nancy Tuckerman whether she thought Jackie would object to her publishing it. Nancy told Nan it would be better if she let it go to another publisher. Refusing to take no for an answer, Nan called Jackie on Martha's Vineyard. When Nan described the passage from the novel, she heard a short, sharp intake of breath at the other end of the line. She accepted that as Jackie's answer to her question. This probably came from an overabundance of enthusiasm and Nan's belief in the merit of D. M. Thomas's book, but it also shows not everyone at Doubleday was protecting Jackie from her history.

On the other hand, I can remember a moment from sitting in Nan's office after she'd read the complete first draft of my book. We had few areas of disagreement. She did take issue with one point. I'd written that Jackie's wishing to publish material from the private life of Fred Astaire, against the wishes of his widow, was hypocritical. Jackie had gone to court to protect her own privacy. Why would she dispense with a similar objection from Astaire's wife? Nan allowed me to go ahead with what I wanted to say, but she also said she agreed with Jackie and not with me. She would've done exactly as Jackie had done. Nan told me that she too wanted to publish biographies with revelations of private life, but she didn't want anyone doing that to her life. "The problem is, I identify with her," she said to me. She was sitting on a raw silk armchair. She'd been downgraded in one of the recent publishing consolidations. She no longer had a corner office. She was still the personification of elegance and candor. The essence of the rivalry between the two women was not that they were different from one another, one famous globally, the other famous in the publishing world. It was that they saw many things exactly the same way. Both of them wanted their private lives protected. Both of them wanted to be fierce and hard-hitting in the biographies they brought out about others. There was nothing demure or ladylike about the searching editorial instincts they shared.

There was something Nan did want out of my book. I removed it, though I thought her objection almost ostrich-like at the time. I had in my first draft a chapter on Jackie and class. It seemed natural to devote a chapter to this. Nan looked at me and laughed. "But that word's so vulgar!" She meant that she would never say of a woman at a debutante party, "she's a classy lady." Nan would never say of sending someone's daughter to Miss Porter's "it'll give her some class." Those are two uses of the word that have in them envy of fancy parties and swanky schools. If you're born to privilege, as both Nan and Jackie were, a key unspoken rule is you never talk about it. That's an attribute of your class.

It may be not unlike white people who never talk about race as an issue. That's part of the privilege they've inherited. They don't see it as a problem. It may be more unconscious for them than in the question of class Nan was flagging. It may be nearer to straight people who won't mention queer people because it's in bad taste. Their silence on sexualities different from their own is an attribute of their power in the world, and their choosing not to speak about it is an exercise of that power. Both Jackie and Nan had the power that came from elite family backgrounds. Nan wanted the word "class" out of my book because it was her instinct that social power should be veiled, and not to veil it would render the book vulgar to other elite readers.

Class as a term of historical, literary, and sociological analysis has been used in American universities at least since the First World War. Most undergraduates have to read original texts by Karl Marx. This isn't because the idea is to turn them into revolutionaries, but because Marx's socio-economic notion of class conflict forever changed ideas about human society starting in the mid-nineteenth century. I couldn't quite believe that Nan, who'd been participating in the center of high-level book discussions for decades, wouldn't take that word as simply a given. I rewrote the chapter to say the same thing, but in different terms. It was one of the times when I realized that editors, even famous ones at major publishing houses, could be more superficial than professors. I'd always regarded the world of universities as somehow inferior to the world Jackie and Nan inhabited. Academics generally have little interest in reaching a broad general audience. They're paid little. They're often proud of their contempt for the commercial considerations that dominate the rest of the world. Now I appreciated how it was possible for an academic view to be superior to the rules of Nan's and Jackie's world. I'd come to this project to investigate Jackie and to find my admiration for her grow. Along the way my admiration for Nan grew too. Now they were both teaching me to respect where I'd come from more than I previously had. They both lacked the intellectual self-criticism and probing analysis that are commonplace among academics.

Still, Nan was more substantial than the string of pearls that came down to her waist. Her curiosity about books and ideas kept her going long past the time when others would have quit. There was always a lightness of touch about her voice, her laughter, and her way of dealing with business reverses that struck me as her shield against anything bad happening to her. Nan was probably the closest I ever came to finding out what Jackie was like in person. Like many intense readers, there was a certain shyness about both Nan and Jackie. Their elegance was wonderful to look at, but it could also convey something like "don't touch me" and "please stand back." It set them apart from other people. They were both more comfortable that way than they would have been in a crowd. Neither of them wanted to be like Bill Clinton out hugging and shaking hands. They both had ways of making most of the people they met unafraid of them, but the true Nan once revealed something to me that I think must have been true of Jackie too. Nan said she didn't really like night life or celebrated restaurants. "I'm really just happiest sitting at home with a tuna sandwich and *Masterpiece Theatre*."

Knowing something about Nan sometimes casts an unflattering light on Jackie. Rivals always have an interest in collaborating. Their interests are the same. Their passions are usually the same. Their talents are too. Rather than keeping her distance from Nan, as Jackie did, she probably ought to have let down her guard, humbled herself, and tried harder to be Nan's friend. When Jackie first went into publishing, before they both arrived at Doubleday, someone they both knew set up a meeting between the two of them. If Jackie wanted to learn the job, the friend told her, Nan was the person who could teach her the most. Instead, when they sat down at a restaurant on 60th Street in the 1970s, the two women were shy with one another.

Nan recalled their talking about their children. That was more Jackie's loss than Nan's. It was an opportunity Jackie let slip away.

Because Nan Talese, Jackie Onassis, and Nancy Tuckerman were all near my mother's age, they all reawakened memories of my mother in me. She'd been gone a long time by the time I met them and wrote my book. In getting to know Nan Talese, even for a little while, I was revisiting all the pleasures and sense of protection I had when I was a child. My mother read me *The Little Engine That Could* at bedtime. Later she read everything I wrote with care and attention. She was so pleased with nearly everything I did that I can never get enough of the like of her again.

Nan renewed that feeling while I was writing *Reading Jackie*. She gave me a sense of security even when she pointed to pages that needed re-writing. All three women were able to work wonders when they were operating in that maternal register, even though none of them looked remotely maternal, and Nancy never had children. Getting to know Nan may have given me an idea of how Jackie missed opportunities in her publishing career, and indulged in a needless rivalry, but I still have the sense that Nan, Jackie, and Nancy—all three of them—were adaptable and unflappable. They were equal to all the difficulties that both work and life put in their way. Knowing something of their example gives me the courage to start on my own penciled list of things to do.

3 A Waspish Novelist

Louis Auchincloss was one of the better-known writers Jackie Onassis commissioned to write for her. He was the author of more than sixty books, mainly novels, but also works of history, essays, and memoirs. Somehow, he also found the time to practice full-time as a lawyer for much of his career. At one of his law firms they were so proud of having been lampooned in a *New Yorker* cartoon as "a Louis Auchincloss style law firm" that they framed it and gave it to him at his retirement. The American Academy of Arts and Letters admitted him as a member in the 1960s, a major honor for a writer. Auchincloss's fictional accounts of old money in New York were accurate and many of them sold well.

I wrote Louis Auchincloss in the fall of 2008 to ask to speak to him about his work with Jackie. Auchincloss's father was a cousin of Hugh D. Auchincloss Jr., who married Jackie's mother Janet as her second husband. So there was also a distant family connection between them. He telephoned me and we had a preliminary conversation before we met in New York. The purpose of the call was really just to ask for the in-person meeting when I'd be in New York in a few months' time, but it ended up going far longer than that. Like many aging men, he was a little garrulous. It's as if their time to tell you everything they have to say is diminishing, so they try to cram it all in while they've got your attention. He was 91 at the time of our call. I was surprised to discover he also had a bit of a chip on his shoulder about Jackie, and possibly about her children too.

Auchincloss had what I assumed was a Yankee, two-syllable pronunciation of "yeah" to sound like *Yay-ah*. There was also a sharpness about the way he spoke. He reminded me of a jeweler, a cutter of precious stones, someone who doesn't make mistakes or have doubts. He told me he'd sold all his letters from Jackie. After her children sold Jackie's personal effects at the Sotheby's sale in 1996, "I thought, well, if they don't care about anything, why should I?" He kept a few letters she wrote after his wife died, but the rest he sold. He added proudly, almost as if it would serve them right, "For a lot of money!" Auchincloss says frankly in his memoirs that he always cared, even from boyhood, about who had money and who didn't. He even confesses that this humiliated his parents, who thought his snobbery was embarrassing. Like Nan Talese, they would have preferred him not to talk about it. Knowing who has what and how much things cost was a feature of what he was like in his nineties too. His selling Jackie's letters, however, concealed something that he told me later. He loved more about her, and the cachet that came from knowing her, than he was ready to admit at first.

He liked talking about people who were greater snobs than he was, or people who aimed to insult him and failed. Auchincloss wrote a historical commentary on Versailles for a book of photography that Jackie commissioned. Deborah Turbeville, a fashion photographer known for her misty, brooding, and atmospheric pictures, was taking pictures of the back rooms at Versailles. She was photographing the cellars and the stables, all the places that were off limits to tourists. Auchincloss contacted Gerald Van der Kemp, who'd masterminded the restoration of the palace after the Second World War. Van der Kemp had immediately begun with a put-down. "What do you know about Versailles!" This was Auchincloss's moment of glory. "Well of course he didn't want to let me in the place, but with Jackie's name the doors *flew* open!"

Auchincloss was alive to social nuances. He liked putting distance between himself and the fashionable people in Jackie's circle. When I asked him what he remembered of Deborah Turbeville, he said "I knew her hardly at all. She's very hard to know. She came to a party we had for the book when it was ready. It was sort of six to eight p.m. She came at eight! Which was when I left." He added, "She was very remote."

Just when I was beginning to dismiss Auchincloss as an amusing social observer with zero substance, he said something that woke me up. I asked him what sort of text Jackie wanted from him.

Her idea was that his text should be something straight and literal. It should tell what was going on at Versailles in an encyclopedic way without particular interpretations. The adjacent pictures would show an artist's appreciation. "Jackie liked the idea of a contrast between something that was completely literal and something that was completely imaginative." Here he revealed something about Jackie's editorial judgement. She wasn't afraid to combine an apple with an orange on the same page. That would lead to a more unusual and unexpected book. When I told him he'd just taught me something about her creativity as an editor, he replied, simply and without fanfare, "She had beautiful taste."

When I asked him whether he had known her before he worked with her, he said yes. He told me the story of a Washington dinner party in the early 1950s. He and his brother had invited Jackie's mother and stepfather to their house for dinner. Janet and Hughdie had said "Jackie's with us," so the brothers said "Bring her too!" After dinner Auchincloss sat down in a corner with Jackie Bouvier, as she was then. She wanted to talk to him about his new novel, *Sybil*, just published in 1951. He told her it was a story about a woman who led a very dull life. "Like mine!" said Jackie. They joked she should be called Sybil Bouvier. While they were talking, Auchincloss, had a strange premonition. This Jackie Bouvier was not going to have a dull life. She was going to be somebody very important. Although she was good looking and pleasant, there were a thousand girls like her. As if he'd seen a ghost, he suddenly realized she was going to be extremely special. It was as if Auchincloss had his own magic intuition to compete with the mystical photography of Turbeville. He would not have me writing him down as the one who was always the literal, unimaginative person in the equation.

This also sheds an interesting light on Jackie. Here she was at twenty-two seeking out an author and asking him to explain his book to her long before she became an editor. Her describing her life as dull also hints at a speck of inferiority in her self-image. She had just announced her engagement to John Husted. In honor of this the two brothers opened champagne at dinner. She later broke off the engagement. It was neither a dull nor an uneventful time in her life. Her calling herself dull and uninteresting was probably more than just social self-deprecation. Other events reveal this too.

Auchincloss had another agenda for our conversation. "To explain my relationship with her: why during the time she was in the White House did I never see her?" I hadn't asked him that, but I was ready to listen if he wanted to tell me. "And why was I never invited to the White House? I think I know the answer. Jackie's was a visual mind. And if she didn't see you, you didn't exist. I talked to some other people who were very hurt, thinking she'd dropped them. She hadn't dropped them: she hadn't seen them. And I think that was it, because after the assassination, she moved to New York and her attitude was sort of 'Where have you been?' I think that was it. Then I saw her quite steadily. And I had before he was elected president." That was his starting position. He'd revise it later, as if it were something that people had teased him about at dinner parties. He was self-conscious about it.

He also returned to an off-color and awkward joke. He'd written a history of Tiffany for Jackie. A great nephew of the founder of Tiffany gave parties in New York at which the most beautiful women of the season were photographed. Auchincloss thought the great nephew and his parties were both boring. "It is a relief to turn from the contemplation of Tiffany's balls," he'd begun one sentence. Jackie had flagged "Tiffany's balls" in his text. "Do you think we might use another word here?" It was a funny joke, but something in my inner ear suggested that Auchincloss was telling it to me because I was a man. He wanted us to have a joke about testicles together. That's what occurred to me anyway. I may have been wrong. Why tell it twice?

Auchincloss also wanted to knock his rivals on the head. Jackie commissioned Olivier Bernier to write several biographies of eighteenth-century figures at Versailles. Bernier also spoke on art to audiences at the Metropolitan Museum of Art. "He's a lecturer on the most luxurious ships. All the rich women in New York go on cruises with him. They adore him. He's not a very profound historian." I wondered why Jackie would put up with a fussy old man like Auchincloss and indulge his pettiness about Bernier. Why choose the two of them when there were so many other well-known historians of France writing for large audiences in America? Was Jackie no better than a rich woman who wanted to go on a cruise with Olivier Bernier?

I promised to send Auchincloss the notes I'd made of our conversation. He could revise or edit them as he liked. Then we'd re-connect in person in New York. He told me "I don't go anywhere because I broke my back and I'm supposed to be recovering. But I think I've recovered as far as I'm going to. I get out and I go around, but I don't do any travelling. I'm rather wobbly if I walk more than a few blocks. But I have a cane and I go around. I go out for dinner."

This made me revise my opinion of him. Just as with Nan in her jumpsuit, this gave me a picture of the sort of old man I'd like to be too. He was someone who could overcome a major injury, be philosophical about the limitations it placed on him, and still take his cane to go out to dinner. If I've made him sound like an unbearable snob, I haven't conveyed that there was also something refreshingly outspoken and honest about him. He wasn't guarded. He shared his hurt feelings with me at never having been invited to the Kennedy White House. If he cared too much about money, it was probably because this covered up some deeper and more private insecurity that had been with him since he was little. When I hung up the phone, I found he'd exhausted me, but I was also looking forward to talking to him again, seeing where he lived, and finding out what he looked like in person.

A few months later, in March of 2009, I was in New York. We agreed on a time for me to visit him in his apartment: eleven a.m. at an address on Park

Avenue between 89th and 90th. I'd never been in a Park Avenue apartment before. The 1960s TV situation comedy *Green Acres* had given me my only idea of what one might look like. It turned out that he lived in a massive, pre-war building. It was a cold spring day with bright, lengthening sunshine, but wintry wind. The front door opened on to a long, mirrored foyer with floor tiles in a black and white checkerboard pattern. There were two doormen, one sitting at a computer. They sent me up to the fourteenth floor without calling him first. One mentioned that Auchincloss was behind the door on the righthand side. Only two apartments per floor. On fourteen I stood for quite a while in a tiny corridor outside the elevator, decorated with his wife's wall painting. She'd painted in a picture of the two of them on a park bench on the lower righthand side.

A handsome young man, possibly a personal trainer, let me in and asked me if I'd rung twice. I said yes, but he didn't apologize for no one's having answered the first bell. He gave me a firm handshake and left, motioning toward the living room, "He's in there." Another entrance hall of checkerboard tiles, but these seemed to be linoleum, not marble. I glimpsed a Black woman, not in uniform, vacuuming, mostly in other rooms. This went on throughout the time I was there. He never mentioned her nor were there any introductions.

Auchincloss was sitting in a comfortable chair in front of a big pair of windows. They had old fashioned Venetian blinds. The room faced north.

There were two groups of seating, a peach striped sofa next to him, where he said I should sit. There was another rust-colored velvet sofa across the room. There was a painting of a Versailles interior in yellow. Auchincloss said it was by an eighteenth-century painter, Jean-Marc Nattier, but he also told me the authenticity was disputed. This was the same trope as Nancy Tuckerman doubting the origins of her Léon Bakst pictures. A contemporary landscape was over the fireplace with at right, badly framed, a photo of an oil portrait of him. He told me the original was on a top floor of the staircase at the Century Club, of which he'd once been president. As with Nan and Gay Talese's house, it felt as if it had been professionally decorated many years ago. It had aged. Fashion in interior design had moved on. His décor was caught in amber. It seemed to be a 1960s or 1970s Park Avenue, but humbler and more lived in than the one Eddie Albert and Eva Gabor had in *Green Acres* when I was a kid.

Auchincloss had on a pair of khaki trousers, British lace-up leather shoes, a blue shirt, and a navy sweater. There were some crusts and stains of food on the front of his sweater. He smelled vaguely of pee. I'd read some of his books after our telephone call a few months earlier. He admired the worlds of Henry James, Edith Wharton, and Marcel Proust, but he didn't have their detachment or their irony. I imagined him as someone who had volumes of *Debrett's*, the *Almanach de Gotha*, and New York's *Social Register* on his reference shelves somewhere. He'd want his own copies. He wouldn't be satisfied with consulting them in a library. In person he seemed like an amateur and a phony, but in time I would come to revise that judgement, just as I had before.

He said that Jackie worked under certain disadvantages. She was an editor who was also the world's most famous woman. People would do anything for her. Also, "she worked only three days a week and you can't get to be a great editor that way." He wanted to establish his independence from her, almost his superiority to her from the start. Then he made the same criticism of her that people often made of him. The Onassis marriage showed that she cared too much about money. Someone had remarked about the time of the wedding in 1968, "I knew the Bouvier girls cared about money, but I didn't know they cared that much." This was a line in a play he had seen. It had the biggest laugh of the evening.

Did Lee's marriage to Michael Canfield, the adopted son of Cass Canfield, publisher of Harper & Row, suggest that both women were interested in writing? Auchincloss replied "Michael Canfield was not considered a great match *a-Tall.*" Cass had a lot of money but was not going to give it to this son, rumored to be the bastard son of a peer. "I can't exaggerate how unimportant he was." He also said Lee was "a dummy." Jackie was not dumb. He thought Jackie's marriage to Onassis had dissolved quite early. He remembered they were "already on the outs" when he ran into Jackie in New York soon after the marriage. "Are you going to keep your name?" he asked her, which, if he did say it to her, was a snide thing to say. He gave the impression of someone waspish and feline. Did he want to insult Jackie because he wanted her attention? He was still mad about not being invited to the White House? Then he suddenly said something more attractive.

I asked whether she had changed between the young woman he had described in the 1950s and the editor at Doubleday. "She must have changed," he said, "but I'm not sure I know how or where." After a pause, "I didn't know her very well." This immediately won me back. He had an interior moral compass. This told him he mustn't lie, or exaggerate his connection to her, or his opportunities to observe her.

Auchincloss remembered in Jackie's favor that even when she was young she liked Wilmarth Lewis because of his big library and renowned collection of eighteenth-century books. I said Nancy Tuckerman remembered Jackie going over to Lewis's when they were both at Farmington. He asked cautiously if Nancy were still around. I said yes and living in western Connecticut. This led to a diatribe against her. He remembered a social slight over the launch party for his book, *Maverick in Mauve.* This was a diary of the 1890s kept by his wife's grandmother. The diarist was Florence Adele Sloane who was related to the Vanderbilts. Jackie was enthusiastic about publishing it. Auchincloss said he didn't think Nancy Tuckerman had much influence over Jackie. They had decided to have the launch party at the Museum of the City of New York and a small exhibition had been specially arranged. Auchincloss spent $2,000 to have the party. "Johnny Sargent," the CEO at Doubleday, "added a little so there could be proper glasses." Auchincloss had threatened to have paper cups if he didn't. There was an extensive guest list. Everyone accepted. Jackie was to be the hostess. Nancy called at the last minute to say there would be too many photographers there. Jackie would feel as if she were in a fishbowl. She wasn't coming.

Auchincloss told Nancy that he would consider it to be "an act of non-friendship" if Jackie didn't come. He thought Nancy was a "weak reed" and hadn't spoken to her since. When Nancy relayed Auchincloss's anger to her, Jackie did eventually agree to come. She arrived early and stayed late. He concluded you had to know how to treat her and not everyone did. "If you told her she was being a shit," she responded. You had to remember that "she was the only woman on the planet to whom everyone said yes." Sometimes you had to tell her, no. She was too used to doing exactly what she wanted. He was outraged that he had been talked into this party and then she proposed not to come.

I write this all down now as he told it to me, but I think it more likely that the party had been his idea in the first place. He had arranged the glittering guest list. He expected to be given a social boost by his celebrity editor. When he found out she didn't want to come, he gave Nancy Tuckerman hell, not Jackie. When I told Nancy this story, she just said "so like him," and left it at that. Nan Talese also remembered him. She edited one of his books. She couldn't remember why, but something had happened during the process of publishing it that made him very angry with her. Nan just shrugged her shoulders and laughed.

Auchincloss wanted to make sure I understood that Jackie's subsequent celebrity contrasted with the insignificance of her original family. The Bouviers were not really "in" anywhere, Auchincloss said. Jack Bouvier was a liability at any party because he drank too much. After Janet divorced him, Black Jack, who had a perpetual tan like George Hamilton's, did come to Lee's wedding reception. Janet didn't want him there. His response was to ask Janet to dance. He whirled her around the dance floor. Auchincloss loved this story. He lingered on how marvelous Black Jack looked while dancing. Auchincloss described him as "big and sexy." It occurred to me that Auchincloss may have wished he could dance with Black Jack instead of Janet.

Auchincloss remembered a social event at the Metropolitan Art Museum where he'd been able to slight Philippe de Montebello, then the director of the museum. Tables were set up in the big hall. He found Jackie and they walked by de Montebello's table without acknowledging him. Jackie sat at Auchincloss's table when de Montebello would have preferred that she sit with him. Why would the author of five dozen books care so much about making de Montebello envious? Why did he so yearn to have Jackie on his elbow at a party? It was as if Auchincloss had a feeling of being perpetually assessed at less than his true worth and Jackie on his elbow healed that injury.

JACKIE STORIES

Of Maurice Tempelsman Auchincloss said "I don't think they ever slept together. I don't think he was sexy." He "was a perfectly nice," but also "an undistinguished little man with a belly." There was no electricity in the room between them. He didn't know, but his intuition was that they hadn't slept together. Of another of Jackie's boyfriends, Pete Hamill, Auchincloss was more enthusiastic. "Now *he* was an attractive man. He was the sexiest man ever." Another of her boyfriends Lord Harlech was also good looking. Auchincloss was telling me that he was attracted to Hamill and Harlech, not that Jackie was. He talked of sex several other times. He mentioned a confirmed bachelor who only got married in his fifties. It was well-known to be a *mariage blanc*, a sexless match between an older woman and a homosexual. He may not have been exactly flirting with me, but my gaydar told me he was happy to be sitting there alone with another single man.

Auchincloss wrote an essay for a magazine on what it was like to work with Jackie as an editor. I hadn't seen this before. We got up and spent twenty minutes looking for it in his cabinets in a back room. He had many of his articles and stories in plastic slipcovers filed in three-ring leather binders. We couldn't find it. There was a special binder devoted to his wife's funeral. One of the items showcased was a letter of condolence from Jackie. Its placement in its own special slipcover showed that its value to him was greater, and he himself more sentimental about her, than indicated by his earlier jokes at Jackie's expense.

I asked him to sign a copy of *Maverick in Mauve* for me. I brought it along with me. He struggled with a black fountain pen. "This is a bad pen," he murmured. Then, "This is a terrible pen," out loud. Then he thought of a camp question. "Shall I sign Louis Auchincloss or Florence Adele Sloane?"

When I told him I shouldn't bother him anymore and it was time for me to go, he stopped me in the hall. He wanted to show me a little framed print of ladies in a carriage, the Empress Eugénie and some friends. He'd meant to give it as a gift but kept it. In one of his memoirs *A Writer's Capital* Auchincloss tells the story of how his Yale roommate once came to stay with him and his parents. They were both in New York to attend a wedding. The young man had committed suicide by falling—backwards and intentionally—out an open window at a party. This followed Auchincloss's having left the man a curt note. The friend had replied wanting him to know that he was not killing himself because of Auchincloss's short-tempered note, but simply because he couldn't go on. He had two impossible crushes at the time he killed himself, one of them on a man. Auchincloss decided in a later memoir the man was gay.

As with Nancy Tuckerman, it's too neat to say that Auchincloss himself was gay, that denying this was at the root of all that made him so conscious of social class and so domineering about it. He'd had trouble facing up to exceptional problems. He'd never been any good at sports. At Groton and Yale, the centers of whatever establishment America had in the 1950s, he wasn't much respected. He'd had years in the navy during the war where his men hadn't liked him either. He'd had a university friend, one of the few men Auchincloss had allowed himself to grow close to, who'd committed suicide. He'd taken refuge in encyclopedic knowledge of New York's four hundred first families a century ago. This was no longer a route to social prestige in America. The Bouviers the Kennedys, and the Fitzgeralds, who were nothing much when compared to the old New England families, had performed remarkably in their lives. They'd outclassed the Vanderbilts and the Delanos in his reference books. Now he was alone and delaying my departure, a stranger who was nothing to him, by commenting on works of art in the hall. I felt his loneliness. He was well aware that though he'd wanted to carry on the stories begun by Henry James and Edith Wharton, his sixty books wouldn't save him from being considered always a little mediocre as a writer. He'd kept his eye on the people and the manners of the past. He didn't care for men who stood in tee shirts on a stage bragging about what an iPhone could do. He cared for Empress Eugénie. So did I. I identified with him.

What he taught me about Jackie was that her taste, beautiful as it was, wasn't always above the level of ordinary rich women who moved in the orbit of the Met. She said when she began redecorating the White House that she was interested in acquiring the best: the best of the period furniture that fit with the era of the building's construction, the best historic advice for restoring the state rooms. I'm sure she would have said that's what she was looking for as an editor too, the best manuscripts by the best authors.

Louis Auchincloss wasn't the best historical or architectural authority on Versailles, nor was he ever going to be the latest word on American social history of the 1890s. There were a dozen experts who were doing more cutting-edge research on France than he was and writing about it for wide audiences. That includes people like Robert Darnton, Lynn Hunt, Simon Schama, and Natalie Davis. Jackie didn't seek them out. She settled for predictable old standbys well-known at the Met. Despite their name recognition in New York none of their books sold well. Jackie was also willing to cancel her appearance at a publishing party for one of her own books at the last minute. She let Nancy Tuckerman take the author's anger on the nose rather than taking it herself. She only decided to come when he threatened to make a fuss. That's not really the kind of editor any writer wants.

It was hard not to like Louis Auchincloss at least a little. He could puncture his own pomposity with a surprise admission about himself. He could also admit to an intense relationship with a gay man in even though he was born in an era when all that was strictly forbidden. I forgot the food crusts on his sweater. I lost track of the time sitting with him and that's one of the best things you can say about any human being. He died the year after we spoke, in 2010, at the age of 92. I hope that wherever he is now, he gets to dance occasionally with Black Jack Bouvier and ride in her carriage with the Empress Eugénie.

4 A *Vanity Fair* Insider

The difficulty in talking to anyone who knew Jackie at all well was getting them to speak candidly. There was often a lot of pro-Jackie gush. There were often declarations of how wonderful she was, how marvelous, how easy. Too few people recollected things she did badly. Few people are that good. I knew I wasn't getting the full picture.

When Jackie was alive the comedian Gilda Radner had several routines in which she made fun of Jackie. In one she was a weight lifter in a pink suit with Jackie's signature sunglasses. In another she fell to her hands and knees on the floor at the sound of a simulated gun shot. Radner was an ace at performing jokes in terrible taste. She expertly probed the symbolic power Jackie acquired in American culture.

All good jokes have something true in them. Jackie became a semi-sacred figure after she survived the murder of JFK. Then when she married Onassis, she left behind a realm of divinity, martyrdom, and self-sacrifice. She became the opposite, a hedonist, a lover of material things, someone who embraces pleasures sure to lead to hell. It was like lifting up the cloak of a saint and finding her wearing black lace underwear. The second marriage amplified Jackie's worldwide renown. The two events joined together to create the fascination with her that still endures. The truth in Gilda Radner's joke was to say Jackie isn't an angel or a devil. She's neither virgin nor whore. She's only human.

This kind of humor was never on display when I was meeting people who knew Jackie. Rather, women especially tended to erect a silent, defensive shield around Jackie. They wanted to protect someone they regarded as vulnerable. It was as if they were a band of Vestal Virgins who wanted to protect Jackie's privacy, Jackie's cult, Jackie's flame. There was often an angry or injured refusal to meet me, as if to say, how dare you write this book that my dear friend Jackie would never have wanted to be written? The former Doubleday editors, Lisa Drew, Shaye Areheart, and Lindy Hess, to all of whom I had good introductions via their former colleagues, were in this category. All of them sent me email or passed on messages that had some suppressed indignation between the lines of their refusal to talk to me.

I had an additional connection via mutual friends to Lindy Hess. She was also still in touch with Nancy Tuckerman at a time I saw Nancy often. So when Lindy Hess emailed to say she wouldn't talk to me about Jackie, I replied. Not to write about Jackie would be like historians making a mutual pact not to write about Queen Victoria. How would that help generations of the future understand Jackie as a significant figure of our times? Hess didn't reply, even though Nancy told her it was okay for her to talk to me. Hess told my mutual friends that I was a difficult character.

When I met the writer and one-time *Vanity Fair* editor-at-large, Sarah Giles, I thought I'd discovered someone who was more willing to talk. She came from a distinguished background. Her father Frank Giles was an important figure in British journalism. He rose to be the editor of one of Britain's most prominent newspapers *The Sunday Times*. Giles caused a sensation when he published in 1983 some newly discovered Hitler diaries. The diaries later proved to be fakes. Giles had to resign. Sarah Giles's mother, Lady Kitty, was from an aristocratic family and descended from a man who'd once been Lord Byron's boyfriend. Sarah worked at *The Tatler,* a nearly defunct British society magazine turned around by its editor Tina Brown. She made it into one of the hottest monthlies in London. Brown then brought Giles to work at *Vanity Fair* in New York during its heyday. Giles was part of the magazine's transformation into the most successful combination of news, photography, politics, crime reporting, and art that has existed for a long time in the States.

Tina Brown had a reputation for sharp elbows and being rude to all but the most bold-faced names, and sometimes even to them. Nor, according to Giles, did Tina Brown always learn the names of all the people who worked for her. Brown didn't come into the office saying "Good morning," because she didn't know who everyone was. Giles ran interference for Brown and soothed hurt feelings. Tina Brown certainly admired Sarah Giles. She had the most enviable collection of contacts of any of her editors. Brown says in her *Vanity Fair Diaries* that Giles couldn't necessarily write, but she could produce good writing and good reporting better than almost anyone else she knew. Brown also felt nervous at the prospect of losing Sarah Giles when the owners of *Interview* magazine nearly poached her from *Vanity Fair*. They wanted Giles to be their new editor, but ultimately chose someone else.

When Fred Astaire died in 1987 Tina Brown saw it as a news opportunity. She assigned Sarah Giles to talk to Astaire's friends for a feature article about their memories of him. Jackie saw this article in the December 1987 issue of the magazine. She telephoned Giles cold in her office at *Vanity Fair*. Giles picked up her phone and heard a whispery voice begin "This is Jacqueline Onassis ..."

"And I'm the fucking Queen of Sheba," interrupted Giles. "Who's this really? I'm busy."

The voice on the other end of the line persisted. She wondered whether she'd have any interest in expanding her article on Fred Astaire into a book. Giles, chagrinned, slowly realized her mistake and apologized. "Don't worry about it," said Jackie. "It happens all the time." Sarah soon had a book contract arranged by a top agent in New York, Mort Janklow. The book was scheduled for publication in 1988.

By the time I met Sarah Giles in 2009, she was back in London. After almost a decade at *Vanity Fair*,

Tina Brown had fired her, as she did many other staff members she once admired. Brown was always looking for new talent and jettisoning the old without regrets. Giles was living in Stockwell, a gentrifying neighborhood in south London. Her apartment was in a former hotel. Her living room had once been a ballroom with a domed ceiling. It was an amazing space. Sarah Giles herself was friendly and blonde, with an upper-class accent and a few extra pounds around the middle. She wore a velour tracksuit with a fake fur trim, and a cast from a recent knee operation. She had the British way of charming by exaggerating to ridiculous extremes. "You find me staggering around," she said on my coming through the apartment door, which she'd left open, and showing me her cast. She didn't want sympathy, she wanted laughter. I felt relaxed with her right away. She knew what she was doing.

We sat down in the kitchen. She began recalling the years "I worked for that dirty rag, *Vanity Fair*." She didn't think it was a rag any more than I did. She knew it would make me laugh again and she was right. What I didn't realize was that Giles's willingness to say many critical things of *Vanity Fair* and Tina Brown concealed her unwillingness to say anything critical about Jackie.

She remembered several of Jackie's unique contributions to her book. Jackie wanted Sarah to expand her magazine piece by talking to some of Astaire's non-celebrity friends. What did his housekeeper have to say? His doctor? The man who made his shoes? Astaire had married only twice. His first wife died young and there was a long interval before he married again, late in life. Jackie was sure he must have had affairs. She insisted that Sarah find out. "What about Cyd Charisse?"

As they worked together, Sarah Giles told me she found herself beginning to feel protective of Jackie. When she sat down in Jackie's apartment for a working session, Jackie never said "Oh Sarah, you won't tell everyone what I've got on my dining room table, will you?" She called upon Giles's loyalty by *not* asking. She never warned Giles to keep the details of her private life quiet. She silently trusted in Sarah's discretion. Jackie won more complicity by using this approach, both with Giles and with colleagues at Doubleday, than she would have by using the British royal family's approach of asking everyone to sign a non-disclosure agreement. Women felt particularly called upon to protect Jackie's privacy by her not asking, men less so.

Sarah's boss, however, wasn't having it. She wanted Sarah to collect every private detail she could about Jackie's life. Once the Astaire book was done, Tina Brown wanted Sarah to write a big feature on Jackie for *Vanity Fair*. Sarah refused. She believed that Tina Brown never understood the American obsession with Jackie. Nor did Tina think highly of Jackie. That's why Tina was willing to be aggressive to get a good story on her, with or without Jackie's cooperation.

Jackie wouldn't allow *Vanity Fair* to manipulate her. Tina Brown threw big parties for Giles's Astaire book in both Los Angeles and New York. She expected Jackie to pose for photographs at these parties to support the magazine. "Jackie didn't come near them," said Sarah proudly. This was the first indication that something was slightly wrong in Sarah's story. Writers who have worked hard on a book inevitably feel at the very least miffed if their editor won't come to the book party. Louis Auchincloss's angry reaction when he learned Jackie wasn't coming to his party was much more typical than Sarah Giles's. Why was Sarah more interested in protecting Jackie's privacy than in winning justifiable attention for her first book, which she'd had to produce on an extremely tight deadline?

The book on Astaire had some troubles coming to publication. Robyn Astaire, a prizewinning jockey and forty years his junior, was Astaire's last wife. She would not cooperate with Sarah as she wrote her book. She sued Giles, Jacqueline Onassis as editor, and Doubleday for the invasion of her privacy. Jackie let Doubleday's lawyers deal with Robyn Astaire's suit. In the end they managed to go ahead without her. Jackie had been involved in repeated court battles about the invasion of her own privacy by Ron Galella. Her daughter Caroline published a book on the law about privacy, possibly to strengthen her family's hand in dealing with an outside world that was too curious to know more about them. Jackie insisted on Sarah Giles's unearthing whatever secrets could be found about Astaire's love life, while she used every weapon she could to prevent writers and photographers from touching aspects of her life she didn't want uncovered.

It's a hard case to decide. Robyn Astaire wasn't a perfectly innocent victim in this story. She later sued to prevent a Fred Astaire and Ginger Rogers movie clip being aired at a Kennedy Center event. She allowed it to be shown inside the auditorium for an evening honoring Ginger Rogers, but she successfully prevented its being shown in a TV broadcast of the event. Wasn't that a little mean spirited? What possible interest did Robyn Astaire have in not allowing Ginger Rogers to be honored?

At the same time, Jackie herself was involved in threatening a suit against *Vanity Fair*. Faced with Sarah Giles's refusal to write about Jackie, Tina Brown commissioned Ed Klein to do a long investigative article about her. Ed Klein was a journalist whom Jackie knew well enough to invite him to one of her Christmas parties at 1040 Fifth Avenue. He had once been the editor of *The New York Times Magazine*, but he was beginning to make gossip his specialty. He has since written a biography of Hillary Clinton assailed by a wide range of critics for its inaccuracies. Jackie was suspicious enough of Klein in advance of all this to make a slighting remark about him to Giles when they were both at her Christmas party. "Guess who was the first to show up?" she whispered in Giles's ear as they passed in the hall at the crowded party. Ed Klein wrote his article claiming to be one of Jackie's closest friends. Jackie sued *Vanity Fair* for Klein's misrepresentation of himself as her confidante. Her lawyers were able to have material from *Vanity Fair* removed before publication.

Though Jackie may've looked sensationally soft in her clothes, she was engaged in hard tactics to keep her own life private. At the same time, she worked in a media business whose very life blood depended on the revelation of material about celebrities that they didn't wish to have published. No one would want to have lived Jackie's life. She ran the risk every day of having details of her private life exposed. However, it may be time we think of Jackie less as a glamor queen than as a savvy media operator, who also fought hard to maintain all the privileges that accrued to her from birth, wealth, fame, and achievement. She'd taken a job at a publisher where she could help turn celebrity exposés into profit, but cried foul when other publishers wanted to publish celebrity exposés of her. Jackie decided she wasn't going to worry too much about an ex-jockey.

Sarah Giles recalled Jackie never mentioning a word about her suit against *Vanity Fair* the whole time they were working together on the Astaire book. Jackie never said anything resentful of Tina Brown or Ed Klein. She pretended as if everything were fine. Giles believed this was an example of Jackie's manners. She avoided anything awkward. She rose above controversy. She'd put in her time at the White House. She could have treated the job at Doubleday as a sinecure, but she didn't. Giles believed that she worked harder at Doubleday than she had to. She retained her composure throughout.

Tina Brown, on the other hand, remained impatient with all the hagiography around Jackie. She believed Jackie had too often been written about as if

she were a saint. That's why she'd given Klein's article
the irreverent front cover caption "Jackie Yo!" when
it appeared in the magazine. Tina Brown, however,
lived to regret this. She came to be in awe of Jackie's
talent as a put-down artist. Shortly after the
publication of Klein's article, Clark Clifford, assisted
by the diplomat Richard Holbrooke, wrote a memoir.
Clifford was a Washington lawyer and a veteran of
the Kennedy administration. Tina Brown's husband,
Harry Evans, was the new president and publisher of
Random House, which was publishing Clifford's
memoir. Harry Evans and Tina Brown gave a book
party at their apartment. The authors invited Jackie
and she agreed to come. Jackie was at Tina's table for
dinner. Jackie made sure that Tina was listening when
she pointed out to the table that *The New Republic* had
torn to shreds a *Vanity Fair* cover story on
Gorbachev's Russia. Almost every one of the people
I talked to in Jackie's circle were recipients of her
legendary thank-you letters on her distinctive blue
stationery. These brief notes were remarkable for
their wit and their turns of phrase. They were always
treasured and saved by the recipients. After the
Clifford dinner, Jackie did not send Tina a thank-you
note.

During my talk with her Sarah Giles dropped a
lot of names. Of Caroline Kennedy, Sarah Giles said
"I'm very fond of her." The two women had met
when Caroline came to a private sale of Indian goods
in Sarah's New York apartment. I had the feeling
Sarah Giles was telling me something else here.
Caroline is powerful. I count her as my friend. I'm

certainly not going to annoy her by telling you anything negative about her mother. The daughter of Giles's superstar agent, Mort Janklow, was "my closest friend in New York." No, Jackie hadn't come to the *Vanity Fair* launch parties for the Astaire book, but she did come to a much more exclusive lunch at Mortimer's, "where a clothing designer you may not have heard of, Carolina Herrera, also came."

Who reading this right now has never heard of Carolina Herrera?

All this was part charm offensive and part display of social brass knuckles on Sarah Giles's part. She wanted me to write up her interview in a way that was pleasing to her. In the conclusion of our chat came the key to what I now see was going on. I thanked her for all the good material she'd given me. "*I haven't given you anything*" she exclaimed, laughing. Then I saw it. She was pleased with herself. She meant for me to take away this. She'd protected Jackie's reputation as a hard-working editor. The way she demonstrated she was a friend-of-Jackie was by revealing as little that was disobliging as she could about her. The only people meant to come out of the story badly were Robyn Astaire, Tina Brown, and Ed Klein.

When Sarah Giles's book on Astaire came out, two of the most influential reviews were hostile. *The New York Times* and *Publishers Weekly* treated it as a picture book that said little new about Astaire himself. Though she had Jackie and *Vanity Fair* behind the book, it was not enough to make the book a critical success. Nor did it sell well enough for

Doubleday to consider it profitable.

In the period just after I met her Sarah Giles suffered a catastrophic reverse. She had a heart attack and a stroke which confined her to a wheelchair for five years. She died in 2014 aged only sixty-three, the age I am now. I'm sorry this happened to her. She made our interview easy. Yes, I think she stonewalled me, but she was fun to be with. She told excellent stories at her own expense. Most of these interviews, I've come to understand only in retrospect, were struggles for control. The interviewee wants to control the story, a power which the writer will almost always have in the end. Robyn Astaire refused to be interviewed by Sarah Giles because she knew she'd be facing a much more expert interviewer than I was. Probably she'd have to put up with Giles's insinuating questions about her May-September marriage to Astaire. It's no wonder she didn't want to be a part of it.

"It's a dirty business and I'm glad I'm out of it," said Sarah as I got up to go. She was chuckling as she said it, but she may've been more honest when she said it this time than when we first sat down. I do understand Sarah Giles using her social acumen to defend herself from an American interviewer she didn't know. I do understand Jackie using Doubleday's legal resources against Robyn Astaire in order to play the role of a serious editor at a major publishing house. That was the person Jackie wanted to be. I would just argue for an end to naïveté about Jackie's power in the world, which was considerable. She was willing to use it. We have to treat even historical figures we admire with the same critical attitude that we bring every day to information on social media. There is very little fact checking on Facebook or Twitter. Employ your skepticism. Doubt is a healthy quality to bring to the table when you're reading a book on Jackie. I say that now because, at the time, I don't think I doubted what people told me enough. I think Giles would have respected me more if I'd thrown more hardballs at her.

Jackie did a number of other celebrity books. There was the Michael Jackson memoir. There were looks at old Hollywood by David Stenn, who wrote books for Jackie on Jean Harlow and Clara Bow. They were dead so they couldn't object. She worked with Carly Simon and Paul Simon on children's books. This earned Jackie the undying hatred of children's books authors who sold books because of their talents as storytellers, not because they'd earned fame as recording artists. Jackie's best books were not by people who could also be found in *People Magazine.*

One of these remarkable books is by Stewart Udall, a politician who retired from the political scene after service in the Kennedy and Johnson administrations. When he proposed his project to Jackie, Udall's sons were still working in politics, but few people knew the elder Udall was still alive and active. Udall's book, *To the Inland Empire*, has both an intelligent argument and gorgeous photography. Udall showed how the British influence on the origins of the United States has been overrated, while the Spanish origins of the country deserve more attention. This was ahead of its time. Jackie didn't protect her privacy in the editing of this book. She flew out to meet Udall. He took her on a hiking trip covering the terrain in the American Southwest traveled by the conquistadors. She allowed herself to be photographed. When the book was turned in and she considered its text not quite right, she didn't hand it to Doubleday's lawyers or to her assistants. She wrote a long letter herself to persuade Udall to change it. There's an honesty, openness, and political punch to Udall's book missing from the Astaire biography. Nor did Udall guard Jackie's privacy when he talked to me about the experience of working with her. He recalled how she "stood up magnificently" at the time of the president's funeral. Of the Onassis marriage he said simply, in a gravelly voice, "I believe some money was involved." There was a straightforwardness, a plain-speaking quality about him that Giles never had with me. Of the two, Udall wrote the more memorable book.

Sarah Giles could have written a better book if she'd used the intimacy and trust she accumulated with Jackie to say, "Look here, Jackie, my dear. What will really make this Astaire book would be if you would write down what attracted *you* to him in the first place. Say something about how his elegance had an influence on you. Why do you love him and what's your estimate of his legacy now that he's gone? Say it in a foreword. It doesn't have to be very long." That was the real story. Those are the things we all would have wanted Jackie to tell us. If Jackie had written that, it would have knocked Ed Klein, Tina Brown, and Robyn Astaire out of the picture forever.

Jackie had talent as a writer and she knew it. She'd written on photography for *The New Yorker*. She'd written an afterword for one of Peter Beard's books on Africa. She wrote two essays on costume and fashion for Diana Vreeland. She wrote on Grand Central Terminal and a foreword for Michael Jackson. I believe two things injured her confidence as a writer. She had such real admiration for the writing of others that she probably felt she could never compete with them. The other thing was the desire to protect her privacy. It was hard to expose herself in writing at the same time as she masked herself behind dark glasses, trench coats, and silk scarves over her head. That was her armor and she had similar psychological protections of herself in place even when she was at home.

In protecting her privacy Jackie prevented herself from finding her own truth. Writing is ultimately about self-exposure and acquiring self-knowledge. She could have come closer to achieving this if she'd hidden less. The lesson she took from the Onassis marriage was never to put herself in the spotlight again. She marshalled all her resources, legal, financial, physical, and human, to stay out of the spotlight, except on rare occasions, forever afterwards. But as with Black Jack Bouvier's reputation for being a rogue, she was never going to put that genie back in the bottle. It was out and about. Until the day she died, there was always going to be a public ravenous for knowledge about her. Rather than hide behind someone like Sarah Giles, who was also acquiring prestige and *chic* by having secrets to keep about Jackie, it would've been better for Jackie to write about every moment she could remember in which she was wowed by Fred Astaire. If she was willing to write for Michael Jackson, who acknowledged his own debt to Astaire, how much more willing ought Jackie have been to write about Fred Astaire himself? Jackie Onassis and Fred Astaire were two of the essential embodiments of grace in the American twentieth century. That would've been a lasting achievement for him, for her, and for all of us. We may understand Jackie's refusal to expose herself further, but sometimes the only way to heal is to go deeper into the very thing you fear.

5 An Iconic Art Director

When Jacqueline Onassis met Ruth Ansel was it a genuine historical moment? Or was it just two women beginning a working relationship that ripened into a friendship? If they didn't win a war together, as Churchill and Roosevelt did, does it count as history? If they didn't explore galaxies together, as Kirk and Spock did, do they deserve their own show?

We recalibrate history every generation. We're now moving toward a view of the past that is less national than international, less about wars and politics than about gender and sexuality, more about women in private life than about men in public. This unusual friendship is interesting because it had its origins in art, in photography, in books, and in magazines. Historians used to care about cabinet documents and the letters of politicians, but today attention to the media is in the mainstream of our cultural concerns. Moreover, because historians are more interested in non-textual evidence than they used to be, our appreciation has grown for people who are powerful exponents of graphic design and understand the impact of the visual on our daily lives.

The two partners in this friendship both came to

prominence in the 1960s. Ruth Ansel collaborated with well-known photographers including Richard Avedon, Andy Warhol, and Annie Leibovitz. She won important awards for her graphic design and art direction. Ansel's layout of a photo of Jean Shrimpton for the cover of *Harper's Bazaar* in 1965 is one of the century's most recognizable images. She raised commercial design to the level of pop art. Ansel went on to put her imprint on important magazines during the latter half of the century, including *Vogue*, *The New York Times Magazine*, and *House & Garden*. She gave *Vanity Fair* its unusual visual flair starting in the 1980s just as it was becoming the most talked-about magazine in the country. She left to form her own practice and began to be taken seriously by museum curators. Her work became the subject of a special museum exhibition at the Moderna Museet in Sweden. She's also featured in a book, *Hall of Femmes*, which describes what it was like for her to be the first woman doing her job at many of the magazines where she worked.

I first talked to Ruth Ansel in the summer of 2010, when large sections of my book had already been turned over to the publisher. None of what she told me made it into the actual book. I'm writing about her here for the first time. I talked to her again recently to ask her to revisit and to elaborate on what she told me ten years ago. She recalled that the artist Peter Beard first introduced her to Jackie in about 1977. A louche figure from a well-off family who did drugs and sold collage-like photos for high prices, Beard and Ruth Ansel worked on books of his

African photography that they created together. Jackie was standing next to him the night Beard's one-man show, curated by a former *Harper's Bazaar* colleague of Ansel's, opened at the International Center of Photography. Jackie was fascinated by Beard. He was one of the people whom she regarded as a creative genius. Jackie found them all magnetic. Leonard Bernstein, Mike Nichols, Diana Vreeland, and Rudolph Nureyev were some of the others. Ruth's introduction to Jackie via Beard could hardly have come from someone who interested Jackie more.

Ruth Ansel is easy to talk to on the phone. She's disarmingly frank about herself and her insecurities. Her friendship with Jackie stretched over nearly twenty years, but there were gaps. She confessed there was a point when she was putting on weight. "I didn't want to see her. I was embarrassed." Her first work with Jackie was on *The New York Times Magazine.* Ruth designed several pages for the magazine that were excerpted from Diana Vreeland's *Allure.* This also served as publicity for the book's publication. Jackie thanked Ruth when the layouts appeared. She said Ruth would win prizes for her Domenico Tiepolo double-page spread. This was typical Jackie, paying a compliment, but going over the top to make it also a shared joke. Ruth remembered that there had been an unflattering close-up of Maria Callas among the pages. It reminded the two women of Tiepolo. If she was able to rise above her personal history by allowing Vreeland to feature Callas in *Allure,* Jackie was also able to take her revenge in small ways.

Jackie could feed *The New York Times Magazine* content from upcoming books, and Ruth could use her talents to enhance the appearance of the special kind of book that Jackie liked. These books typically had elements of high style and dramatic photography, as well as wisps of autobiography, in some cases all three. Often the autobiography was concealed and only visible to those in the know, or to those who looked carefully. The two women were useful to each other, but there was also an unguardedness about Jackie's manner with Ruth, a conspiratorial quality, that was unlike her other professional relationships. "We will plot and do great things," Jackie told Ruth. Who wouldn't want to work with someone like that, even if she weren't already a legend on seven continents?

When Ruth went to visit her at Doubleday's offices, Jackie was wearing tailored Valentino couture trousers. They were creased in front from sitting in her desk chair. Her silk shirt was partly untucked. Jackie was relaxed about imperfection. She put Ruth at ease by making her sit down and digging an aluminum foil packet out of her bag, saying "You want a carrot?" The two women already trusted each other. They decided they wanted to do a book together. They weren't sure what the book should be. They brainstormed ideas in Jackie's office. This is not the way you usually sell a New York editor on a book unless you're on very close terms with her. Even then, it's rare.

They agreed their book should be on a talented

woman. Ruth remembered Jackie's being interested in the maverick qualities of highly cultured people in dance or music or art. She was drawn to smart, strong-willed women who shattered stereotypes. Jackie herself had refused to be a predictable political spouse. Nor as the widow of a Greek billionaire was she a typical book editor either, though there's evidence that she wasn't willing to acknowledge those maverick qualities in herself.

Ruth thought that Jackie had a split personality at work. She did books on figures of cultural importance such as Martha Graham and Judith Jamison. She also wanted to do commercial books that made money. For these books she was willing to consider more popular subjects. "I think she was able to remove herself from the Jackie Onassis persona that she was protective about," Ruth told me. She was willing to cease to be the woman who brought Nobel prize winners to the White House and featured famous dancers as an editor. She could then "become Onassis the editor who wanted to know about disclosure, affairs, dirt, gossip."

The two women considered Paloma Picasso, Elsa Peretti, Diane Keaton, Ali MacGraw, and Madonna as possible subjects for their book. When Ali MacGraw's name came up, Jackie was instantly struck. She wanted to telephone her right away. Ansel had MacGraw's phone number. They were friends. Jackie got her on the line but found that MacGraw was already committed to another publisher. That impulsiveness of Jackie's, that confidence that when she got someone on the phone, even someone she didn't know, she could persuade them to write a book, is unusual. It's an ambitious, forceful dimension of her, an awareness of the power of her celebrity that is invisible when you look at the retiring pictures of her putting up her collar and turning her shoulders away from paparazzi.

Then Ruth Ansel stumbled on a book idea she was sure they'd both love. She asked Richard Avedon for Audrey Hepburn's telephone number. Hepburn was in Switzerland, where she'd retired early from films. Ansel called Hepburn to ask whether she'd permit her biography to be written. Undoubtedly Ansel also conveyed the name of the editor she was working with as well. Hepburn admitted that, yes, now might be the time to tell some stories for her grandchildren. This was a major coup. To have won the tentative consent of someone with Hepburn's fame is more than half the battle in writing a book about a living person.

Ruth relayed this to Jackie. She expected Jackie's response to be something like "Wow!" Instead, Jackie wasn't interested. She took their conversation in an unexpected direction. She wanted to discuss Audrey Hepburn's marriages with Ruth. Hepburn had been married first to actor Mel Ferrer, and then to an Italian psychiatrist Andrea Dotti. Jackie knew Dotti had given Audrey a hard time and had been unfaithful to her. Jackie also said it was a sad fate for Audrey to have to spend her years after Dotti with the Dutch actor Robert Wolders. Jackie regarded Wolders as "nothing but a gigolo." Why should a woman like Hepburn have to try and make herself interesting for him? Jackie identified with a woman prominent because of her own great talents, stuck in unhappy relationships with male partners.

Jackie turned down her idea because she and Audrey Hepburn were too similar, Ruth concluded. They were women who mirrored each other's style. Ruth made an art director's summary of their appearances: "They both wore Givenchy couture and had the same thin, small-breasted bodies." They both had "large, sculptural, square-jawed, beautiful heads." We tend to be our own harshest critics. Jackie may have simply decided that someone who came from a privileged background, as Audrey Hepburn had, and looked too much like her, who was well-known for her elegance, and who'd had bad marriages wasn't worth having a book written about her. That's what Jackie saw when she looked at Audrey Hepburn. She didn't think of the epic films, she thought of Hepburn's private life that was too much like hers. She didn't want a book about that.

When Ruth moved to become the creative director at *House & Garden,* she and Jackie continued their brainstorming sessions. Jackie tried to help by suggesting ideas Ruth might use in the magazine. It wasn't the houses of the high-born that Jackie suggested for magazine features, but those who had some kind of creative talent. What about the Scottish house of the opera composer Gian Carlo Menotti? They somehow hit upon the Californian house of Lee Radziwill's new husband, the film director Herbert Ross. Jackie wrote it down on her yellow pad for Ruth to take away. She added "Flattery needed."

Jackie invited Ruth to her house on Martha's Vineyard. She didn't do this with everyone. I don't think I've come across any of her other authors being given that privilege. Ruth remembered Jackie's being critical of the architect Hugh Newell Jacobsen's plans for Red Gate Farm. Jacobsen's design had the drive run up to the back door, not the front. It ended at the herb garden, which had been laid out for the convenience of "the help" not the owner. Ruth confessed that she'd been too shy to ask Jackie to see the whole house. Jackie didn't volunteer to show it to her. Ruth observed in Jackie's defense that she was a snob about style, but not about class. "Sure, she loved luxury, especially if made by an inspired creator. That was something we shared. What's wrong with that?"

Jackie wasn't Everywoman. She had millions to spend on an estate, which she had built from scratch on America's most expensive island. She didn't use the British word "servants," but few Americans would speak of "the help" either, especially in the plural, unless they're being ironic. Even people with whom she was on close terms were a little shy with her. That had to have been lonely for Jackie too.

Ruth Ansel remembered also going to 1040 Fifth Avenue. She went for one of Jackie's big annual Christmas parties. For twosomes with Jackie they sat down in front of the fire in the library. Maurice Tempelsman occasionally stopped by to see if they were all right. Ruth wondered whether this was a signal meant to tell her it was time to go. Ansel thought Jackie had genuine affection for Tempelsman and that he was an indispensable companion to her. She also noticed what Louis Auchincloss thought the relationship lacked. "There was no heat between them. He was a caretaker."

Ruth concluded by saying her friendship with Jackie was one of the most profound, life-affirming relationships she had ever known. She added it was also unexpected because her own background was nothing special. Still, Jackie had let her into her circle. When Jackie died Ruth received an announcement of the memorial service. She looked at the engraved card. "I wasn't sure whether this meant I was invited or not, so I called up Jackie's apartment." Jackie's son John picked up the phone. Ruth admitted her confusion to him. John replied "Of course, Ruth. My mother wanted you to be there."

What's most interesting about these two women who helped shape the visual consciousness of the late twentieth-century print media is that they found one another and tried to collaborate. Jackie's choosing Ruth Ansel for intimacy in private contrasts with more famous women about town, who at different eras, were her public friends, Bunny Mellon, for instance. Ruth speaks to the genuineness of Jackie's aspiration to make her mark in the work she did rather than in the places she lunched.

They agreed there should be more books written about women's lives. More than a hundred years ago Virginia Woolf said that there could be no equality between men and women until more history was written about the lives of women. Ansel and Onassis both instinctively understood that point, which was jeered at in the 1920s when Woolf wrote it. Ruth

Ansel was also part of a movement to cease depicting women as happy mannequins for pretty clothes. In her images they appear sometimes depressed, sometimes abstract, sometimes spaced out, and sometimes turned on. Ansel witnessed and helped to make happen the birth of the contemporary notion that fashion can be art. She contributed to the increase in graphic design's prestige such that attending to it has now become one of the ways we read culture as a whole. Ruth and Jackie helped to envision a transformation in the magazine and publishing world that was equal to the change Woolf called for in the literary world.

In our last conversation I gathered the courage to ask Ruth a personal question. Had there ever been any sexual tension in her friendship with Jackie? I told her about what I knew of Jackie's friendship with Nancy Tuckerman. There were other, admittedly circumstantial, bits of evidence that led me to ask. Jackie was friends with the novelist Jane Stanton Hitchcock, one of whose best books has a lesbian as its hero. It describes the world of bored Park Avenue wives who entertain each other while their workaholic husbands are downtown in board rooms with the other boys. Jackie was also friends with Carly Simon, who has sometimes admitted to a degree of bisexuality. There was a pregnant pause on the phone. "Actually," said Ruth. "No." Then she laughed at me. She forgave me for being nosy. She worked with Beatriz Feitler at *Harper's Bazaar.* Bea was certainly a lesbian. She'd once tried seducing Ruth into a three-way with her girlfriend. Ruth wasn't tempted. "I don't know why I wasn't," she told me. "I had plenty of opportunities. Why didn't I?" She laughed again.

Among all the people I talked with about Jackie, Ruth was the most accessible. She didn't hold me at arm's length as some others did. There was something unexpected in her openness. That made me see and also feel why Jackie was drawn to Ruth, wanted to work with her, and maybe loved her too. Jackie might have trusted her friends more than she did. Ruth presented Jackie with a considerable opportunity when she won Audrey Hepburn's consent to a book being written about her. Jackie's turning away from Hepburn may have been self-dislike, or more gently a lack of belief in herself, masquerading as finding Audrey "not all that interesting." It's parallel to Jackie in her twenties telling Louis Auchincloss that he should've named the dull character in his novel Sybil Bouvier, because Jackie regarded herself uninteresting. She had the chance to have the visual style and cultural weight she shared with Hepburn analyzed by a premier practitioner of the visual arts. This feels like another time when Jackie protected her privacy when she ought to have kicked the doors open wider. It would have been better to collaborate with someone she already trusted. Jackie was always chasing after high-flown artistic talent—Menotti in his historic Scottish mansion—when the real story was in the mirror, if she could only be brave enough to tell it.

For all her wishing to do books on women Jackie may have unconsciously remained the prisoner of her upbringing. This upbringing had imperatives that were taught to most American women of her generation. You must never seek to be the center of attention. You must never talk about self. You must never display the sin of egotism. You must never assert the superiority of your point of view when men are present. Jackie might well have learned to say what I know Ruth Ansel would have said of those values. "To hell with all that."

6 A Cultural Buccaneer

I have always loved imagining what it would have been like to live in Jackie's world. My own Jackie fandom begins from the fact that I never could have entered that world. Nor will I ever have presidents at my beck and call, though the truth is she felt used by LBJ, avoided talking to Nixon, and thought Ford was a nice man, though boring. Having gone to a public high school in Columbus, Ohio, as I did, will never be the same as having been to Miss Porter's. Nor at my high school was it permitted to bring your horse as Jackie did. I don't think it was even conceived of. I will never have Jackie's courage or her style. I will never have the grit it took to face the photographers every time she walked out on the street. Even inside wasn't safe. "Aren't you Jackie Onassis?" strangers used to say to her in the elevators Doubleday shared with other corporate offices. "No, I'm not," she sometimes replied.

In writing a book about her, though, I could get close to things she had that I didn't. I could get a feeling for her relationships with other people. I could try and find out what animated her. In recalling some of the interviews I did for that book, I also found that some of the things she had, I definitely don't want. I had an inside look at some of the squabbles, double-crossings, intrigues, and resentments in what passes for high life in America. She had friends in prominent places who were fired at the peak of their careers with no more than a moment's notice. She had a sister with whom she competed, sometimes for extravagant purchases, sometimes for the same men. When she collaborated with famous people for worthy causes sometimes they later proved treacherous. I'm glad she had to deal with all that and not me.

Here's one of those glimpses into Jackie's world. It begins with a woman who was much more successful as a cultural buccaneer than Jackie was. Sailing buccaneers collected pieces of eight, Spanish silver. A cultural buccaneer collects artists and glories in her closeness to them as a pirate loves treasure. Born to a rich family in Philadelphia, Rosamond Bernier was just as ambitious as Jackie was to spend her time near to creative genius. She pursued artists with a flamboyance and a focus that Jackie never mastered. She started young. While Bernier was still in college, she met her first husband. They went to live in Mexico, where Bernier came to know and was even dressed by Frida Kahlo. She went to Paris as a features editor for *Vogue* soon after the war. She sought out and interviewed all the luminaries of the twentieth-century art world, including Picasso, Matisse, and Fernand Léger. She and her second husband founded an art magazine in the 1950s called *L'Oeil,* The Eye. It was high quality content at a low cost. You could even find people reading it in the Métro.

When the marriage ended, Bernier came back to New York. She married as her third husband the British art critic, John Russell, who wrote for *The New York Times.* Zandra Rhodes made Bernier's wedding dress. The legendary architect Philip Johnson threw Bernier a wedding party at his glass house in New Canaan, Connecticut. Andy Warhol, Stephen Spender, and Aaron Copland were all among the wedding guests. Afterwards, Bernier lectured about art to large audiences at the Metropolitan Museum of Art. She would show slides with names and dates and critical theories, but the crowd loved her because she could also throw in personal stories. For example, she remembered watching Matisse while he was sketching. He swore like an auto mechanic. Bernier wore couture dresses at these lectures. She spoke without notes. She adored the spotlight. She was equally a hit at art museums in California and Texas. She gave two hundred and fifty sold-out performances until she retired in 2008, the year before I met her.

It's no surprise then that Rosamond Bernier should have persuaded Jacqueline Onassis to acquire and edit a book she wanted to write. It was to be on Philip Johnson. Bernier had done television interviews with him that brought out the best in a man known both for his arrogance and his secretiveness. Jackie herself had much to expect from a book on Philip Johnson. Her own friendship with him went back at least as far as the 1960s. He'd competed with I. M. Pei and other prominent architects to design the Kennedy Library in Boston. Johnson produced a Kennedy memorial in Dallas in 1970. The two of them collaborated in the saving of Grand Central Station when the railroad wanted to pull it down to build a high rise. She and Johnson both aimed to protect historic buildings in New York. They saw each other frequently at black tie dinners to raise funds for the Municipal Art Society. They were memorably photographed together at one of those dinners. So long as they both lived Philip Johnson and Jacqueline Onassis were two of New York City's megawatt attractions.

I made an appointment to go and speak with Bernier about the Philip Johnson book project. Her building had a doorman, marble floors, a sleek modernist lobby. It was on a narrow, tree-lined street not far from Bloomingdale's. I went upstairs in a silent elevator. When I reached the end of the hall, I found her apartment door was ajar. I knocked cautiously. She called out "Do please come in!" I found her standing in front of a sofa. Her hands were clasped in front of her. She was receiving me as if I were a papal delegation, but she was smiling and looking friendly. It was somehow both stagey and fun at the same time. The apartment was painted all black. "I did it that way to hide the imperfections." There were wide-slatted shades over all the windows, also black. There was a monumental Jasper Johns print over the sofa. She was small, neat, and red-haired. She volunteered her age without my asking, 92. She looked about 65. She had a small pot of tea and a cup and saucer waiting for me on a side table.

She told me her book with Jackie was tentatively entitled, *Being Philip Johnson*. Bernier had done three TV shows for PBS on him. "When I divorced in France, he was protective, and like a brother to me." She came as a single woman to New York after an unpleasant break up. She appreciated Johnson's support. As the material accumulated for the TV programs, she started thinking of a book. She had tapes of him talking which she intended to transcribe, with notes in the margins of the buildings to which he referred in his commentary. Then, as plans were far advanced for the book, and a contract had been signed, she learned that Johnson had given his okay to another author for a book that would directly compete with hers. Johnson told Doubleday he would no longer consent to the publication of Bernier's book. He telephoned neither Onassis nor Bernier to let them know. He let publishing executives at Doubleday pass on the bad news.

This came as a shock. One Philip Johnson biographer describes his relationship with Bernier as among the most civilized of his life. She hadn't quite reckoned with his ruthlessness and his insistence on the highest quality of self-promotion. He probably thought this other book would be better. "He'd only expressed great interest in what I was doing. We were really very close," Bernier told me. She thought a moment and added, "Jackie was very hurt." After another moment she said, "Jackie was furious."

Sitting after lunch one day with Jayne Wrightsman, whose collection of eighteenth-century French furniture is now at the Met, Bernier told her story. Jayne Wrightsman made her promise never to speak to Philip Johnson again. "And I didn't."

Johnson didn't think enough of Jackie as editor or of Bernier as author to carry through with a book in which time and money had already been invested. Jackie liked filling her New York address book with high-octane artistic geniuses, but she also exposed herself to their tantrums and unreliability. It speaks in her favor that not everyone catered to her. She had dealings with people who believed in their own talent more than they believed in her. Most former first ladies confine themselves to uncontroversial isolation. The only real exceptions in the twentieth century are honorable ones: Eleanor Roosevelt and Hillary Clinton. Jackie chose to go perch on I. M. Pei's uncomfortable living-room furniture long after he built her husband's library. She sat in a white plastic armchair inside Nureyev's beach house. For Jackie it was about the company not the comfort.

When the rival book on Johnson came out, according to Bernier, "it sank like a stone." She laughed after she said this, possibly sensing that her wanting revenge was childish. Her husband simply brushed it off as what Philip Johnson was like. He refused to hold a grudge. The crashing and burning of book projects, even those that are far advanced, is par for the course in publishing. Bernier's instinct by the time I met her had moved in the direction of her husband's. In her 2011 memoir *Some of My Lives*

Bernier speaks generously of her friendship with Johnson and, equally generously, omits to mention anything about his being to blame for the cancellation of her book.

Rosamond Bernier had other, happier memories of Jackie and her family. She and John Russell went together to Caroline's wedding in Hyannis Port. She remembered George Plimpton's fireworks show. Plimpton poked fun at the fact that no one really knew what Ed Schlossberg did for a living. "What Ed Does" was one of the fireworks displays as the fog rolled in.

Maurice Tempelsman, Bernier thought, was a "most protective, decent person." Both she and John Russell liked him. They always went out as a foursome for dinner on John Russell's birthday. Even when Jackie was dying, the birthday dinner was still held, but they were only three. Jackie sent a note with Maurice Tempelsman explaining her absence. Jackie once gave John Russell a big print for his birthday, "which is hanging in there, in the bathroom," she told me. I made a note to myself as Bernier talked. Why hang Jackie's print in the bathroom? She was open and willing to talk about everything, but I wasn't always brave enough to ask.

One of JFK's sisters was at the wake for Jackie after she died. Bernier was surprised when she arrived at Jackie's apartment to find the sister saying, "Won't you come in and say a prayer for Jackie?" When she was alive, Bernier remembered, Jackie had a French style of entertaining. If you went to her apartment for lunch, the service was as it would be in France, with a butler or a maid serving. Now after her death, Bernier and John Russell were led up to Jackie's coffin which was standing in the midst of a noisy Irish party. "Very strange. It wasn't Jackie's style at all."

Some years after Jackie's death, when the Met sponsored an exhibition on Jackie's White House clothes, Bernier attended the opening dinner. She remembered sitting between Oleg Cassini and Philippe de Montebello. Cassini was bitter. He thought he had not been given enough credit and Givenchy too much attention in the Met's show. The party was partly in his honor, but Cassini only felt resentment. Jackie was gone, but the sharp elbows, and big egos were still on display among the people to whom she'd given her patronage.

Another person whom Bernier also knew well was Diana Vreeland. "Jackie responded to Diana's flair," said Bernier. Vreeland was forced to leave *Vogue* abruptly in 1971 and had very little money. She was low after Condé Nast fired her. Jackie was one of those who helped collect money to fund Diana's post-*Vogue* special consultancy at the Costume Institute of the Metropolitan Museum of Art. Even that came to an end, however. "Diana lived over in the next street." They both felt ill-used by the world. Vreeland was going blind. "I'd go over to make tea. We'd have vodka. Then another. And feel better."

Toward the end of our time together, Bernier had exhausted her fund of Jackie stories. She wanted to talk about John Russell instead. As he got older, she told me, he developed Alzheimer's disease. This came on gradually. One morning Bernier entered his bedroom.

"Who are you?"

"I'm your wife."

"Are you sure?"

"Yes, I'm sure."

"Marvelous. Let's go to England and tell the family."

Another time they were both in a taxi coming home from the opera. He said to her, "I don't even know where you live. How will I get in touch with you again?"

Once, encountering John Russell in their apartment, he asked Bernier, "Who are you?"

"I'm your wife."

"Are you sure?"

"Yes."

"Well that's wonderful. I'm so happy."

Style, knowledge, sophistication, having been on a first-name basis with Picasso, and the support of Jackie Onassis as your editor don't necessarily bring contentment. You may live in Jackie's orbit and disappointments will still attend you. The man who throws your wedding party may double cross you later. Your husband may develop an incurable ailment. Cultivate the ability to tell stories that make you laugh. There may be vendettas and intrigues underneath, but on top you must stay smiling. You stand and receive the young man in your black apartment as if he were the most interesting person you ever met.

Rosamond Bernier died in 2016 at the age of 100. Spending time with her made me realize this for the first time. It wasn't Jackie's Fifth Avenue apartment. It wasn't her house on Martha's Vineyard. It wasn't riding on horseback across farms in Virginia. None of these were the most important things Jackie had. The people were. The combination of personal experience, of achievement in the world, and of charm like you wouldn't believe was common among the people in Jackie's circle. To spend an hour with any one of them was unlike an hour I'd spent with almost anyone else, and I'd already reached my fifties when I was meeting them for the first time.

The fact that not everyone bowed down to her, that Tina Brown and Ron Galella were out to get her, that Louis Auchincloss was ready to give her an ultimatum, that Philip Johnson walked out on her at the last minute, also increased my respect for her. She didn't win every battle. Nor did she get all the proximity to creative genius that she wanted because she didn't begin by accepting the chance of a youthful appointment at *Vogue* as Bernier had. The stories about this vary. Either her mother stopped her, or she had a bad experience on the first day at work that made Jackie walk away from the opportunity she had of working at *Vogue*. Jackie in later life never specialized and acquired the knowledge Bernier did by founding an art magazine. She never had the reputation for expertise in art that Bernier did because she didn't step forward on a regular basis and lecture about what she knew. She was too retiring, too shy for that. That wasn't in her personality.

Rather, she quietly exploited the contacts she had at the Metropolitan Museum across the street.

She complained when the floodlighting of the new Temple of Dendur poured into her apartment at night. She consulted her own convenience. Much as Jackie admired pirates—her father, JFK, and Onassis were all pirates—she never became the cultural pirate her friend Rosamond Bernier was. I suspect the reason is this. There was too much at stake. There was too much to lose. She kept herself going with her friends and her book projects because she'd once had firsthand contact with what it might be like to lose everything. She had to hold on to serenity, sanity, and stability as tightly as she could. She wasn't going to walk on stage in a beautiful dress and say into a microphone "I remember Pablo Casals." "I remember André Malraux." "This is what I remember about Dallas," because, I think, it might have destroyed her. She never went to visit Philip Johnson's Kennedy memorial in Texas. When Nan asked her about the novel featuring JFK's casket it was a horrible surprise. On occasion she could put herself at a detached, humorous remove from all this. When a Doubleday colleague asked her whether she'd attend an upcoming sales meeting in Texas, she said, "I think I'll pass."

In a very small way, and though she was a shy woman, Nancy Tuckerman *was* willing to take the microphone. She stood up and spoke at my book launches. Maybe Jackie should have gone on stage too. Maybe she should have gone to that sales meeting in Texas. It might have shaken her, but do you think it might also have saved her?

7 An Expert from the Ballet World

Ralph Lauren, Gucci, and Bergdorf Goodman sell it. Wedding magazines and dinner party websites teach it. Young people go into law or medicine or financial services to make the money to keep it or to acquire it. However, in America, where we also tend to believe that, for us, class doesn't exist, it's not that easy. Class is not only the possession of money, as anyone can name half a dozen rich people who are crass. Nor does buying a beautiful outfit necessarily tell you how to speak or to act when you're wearing it. Nor is it only bravery or manners. If it were, emergency services personnel who conceal what they're required to do under pressure every day would rank higher in American society than they do. Maybe the only thing a majority of Americans would agree on is that Jackie had class.

Writing about the history of the British monarchy alerted me to differences between the two countries in ideas about class. Writing the book on Jackie was revealing because I had the chance to meet people who showed me quietly, sometimes contemptuously, often mockingly the distinctive ways class works in America today. One of these people was Francis Mason. When I met him he was in his late eighties. He was a friend of Jackie's from at least the later 1970s through to her death in the early 1990s. She edited one of his books, *I Remember Balanchine*, which appeared in 1991. She commissioned another, *I Remember Martha Graham*, which he was still working on when she died.

Mason was a soldier during the Second World War. He participated in the D-day landings in France. Afterwards he was cultural attaché at American embassies in Britain and in Belgrade. In London he obtained State Department sponsorship for performances by Balanchine's New York City Ballet, Martha Graham, Merce Cunningham, and Alvin Ailey. He later became an assistant director of the Morgan Library in New York. He broadcast dance reviews on the radio in New York City starting in the late 1940s. He edited *Ballet Review*, a magazine meant to reach the sort of outside amateur he was himself when he was first introduced to the dance world. He made friends with two essential figures of twentieth-century dance. He collaborated with the choreographer, George Balanchine, on a book telling the stories of the great ballets. It was a bestseller long before he began to work with Jackie. Mason was also close to Martha Graham. He served on the board that oversaw and funded her dance company for decades. As its chair he guided the company through critical lawsuits after her death.

I was due to meet Mason at two p.m. on a November afternoon in the lobby of his club. I waited an hour. He didn't show up. He called me that evening. His first line surprised me. "I fucked up. I'm sorry. Let me take you to lunch." He asked me to meet him at the club again the next day. He coughed on the phone. I had the feeling that he was unwell but didn't want to talk about it. That was the first thing he taught me. It's okay to use four-letter words when you cause someone inconvenience. Following through on meeting someone he'd promised to see, who was a complete stranger to him, and despite feeling unwell, also seemed an unusual display of gallantry and ignoring whatever was ailing him.

His club was the Century Association. From the outside it was an imposing building. It looked like an American version of an Italian palazzo. It was on a narrow side street in midtown Manhattan. There were no signs outside saying what it was. You had to know. Inside it felt a bit shabby. Some of the walls were lined with cork and burlap, as if they were permanent exhibition spaces. It was founded in the middle of the nineteenth century as a place for artists and writers. The artwork of members was still on the walls, some of it famous and old. Other paintings looked amateurish and recent. The entry hall had a high ceiling and a grand central staircase, but the cork and burlap made it feel the reverse of luxurious. It was as if they were maintaining the fiction that they were all bohemians with zero extra money to spare.

When Mason arrived, I was standing in an alcove reading a newspaper. I didn't notice him. He made no fanfare. He didn't slap my shoulder or make a fuss. He just showed up wordlessly at my side. He was a small man in a brown suit. He had this quietness about him. There was no false heartiness or hail-fellow-well-met manner. He pointed to the central staircase. "I don't do steps anymore." He led me away to the side and took me up in the elevator. We emerged and went into a dining room where the far walls were lined with books. The dining area overflowed into the library. Leather-bound volumes were the main decoration. Nobody was having fancy food with seven locally-sourced ingredients. They were eating plates of cube steak with sides of coleslaw.

Mason recalled having direct dealings with Jacqueline Onassis when he was at the Morgan Library. His immediate boss was the director, Charles Ryskamp. Here's a bit of our dialogue that I recorded. He didn't like my asking for permission to record our conversation. He wrinkled his eyebrows at the small voice recorder I put on the table, but he didn't object.

Francis Mason: "Whom [Ryskamp] you should talk to by the way, also a member here, he was director of the Morgan from something like 1975 to 85, a very agreeable, intellectual Midwesterner, if you can say that.
Bill Kuhn: "I hope I'm one myself."
Francis Mason: "He comes from Michigan!"
Bill Kuhn: "Well, I'm from Ohio."
Francis Mason: "Yes, that *is* worse."

His eyes sparkled. His insult was the first mark of intimacy between us. It wasn't going anywhere or doing anything except to show me I was worth a little playfulness. He was repaying me for the voice recorder. He was taking me more seriously than I was worth.

When Mason was at the Morgan, he knew some of the smaller art house publishers downtown. Probably the Morgan often had reason to collaborate with them on catalogues for their exhibitions. Jackie had just left Viking. She was looking for a new job. She wanted to meet some of these smaller publishers and take a tour if she could. She asked him a favor. Could Mason introduce her? She would bring her car and driver down to the Morgan. She would pick him up. They could go meet several of his contacts in the world of boutique publishing, specialists in upmarket, large format books of art and photography. They invested some weeks in this.

Then, later that year, Mason was surprised when she joined not one of the small places where he'd introduced her, but another of the big publishers. Nor was Doubleday known for artistic book production. If anything they were considered to be a publisher of mass-produced, cheaper books sold in the hinterlands, far from the world of urban connoisseurship. Mason made it seem as if the joke was on him. He was foolish for not having realized it all along. "I suppose they paid her more money." He was repeating in a more elliptical way what a number of her colleagues said about her. She cared too much about money. He would return to this later in the conversation, but for the moment Mason made it seem as if the fault was his. He should have known better. He may have grown up with some money himself, and maybe he could afford to think less about it than she did. Jackie told Louis Auchincloss she was conscious of the vulnerability of a woman from a debutante background. If she had no money of her own, she had to find it through marriage in the era before women could work. She had to sacrifice her independence in order to assure economic well-being. This would certainly have been on the mind of Jackie Bouvier in the 1950s too. She wasn't going to inherit much from her father, nor could she anticipate anything substantial from her stepfather.

It's more likely Jackie went to Doubleday because Nancy Tuckerman was already there than for the salary they offered her. She needed the protection. She didn't tell Francis Mason any of this. She wasn't entirely candid with him. She asked him to help her. Then she did exactly the opposite of what she told him she was intending to do. She didn't give him any explanation.

Mason didn't resent Jackie for this. He did make a point of saying that she was more willing to help the Morgan Library, and later the Martha Graham Company, with her presence than with cash contributions to their ongoing expenses. He was himself president of his club about the time it began admitting female members. Brooke Astor and Jackie were the first who came in after women were invited to join. Mason used a British expression about Jackie, one so pretentious that it sounded as if he were making fun of himself and trying to get me to laugh. He said of Jackie "She had no side!" He meant that she was informal, not standoffish, the reverse of stuffy. "She was calm, cool, collected, and," here leaning across the table toward me he stopped to place emphasis on the word, "*fun*. It's a hard act to follow. She had it all. It was really glorious." Then he dispensed with Lee Radziwill in a single sentence. "Her sister's a bore."

One of the first things Jackie did on becoming a new member at the Century was to break an unwritten rule. "I remember one day coming in and she was sitting on the steps. Sitting on the steps! A lady sitting on the steps. It was charming. Mrs. Astor wouldn't do it. Brooke's been a member for many years. Jackie could do anything." She wasn't going to be the former first lady people expected her to be. She'd rather break rules of decorum that had also excluded women for more than a century.

Mason served twice on the board of directors that raised funds for Martha Graham's dance company. After Martha Graham died, she left all her personal belongings to Ron Protas, a younger companion. Protas interpreted her will to mean that Graham had left him the rights to all her dances. He wanted Martha Graham's company to compensate him every time they performed one of her classic works. Mason led the company's fight against Protas in the courts.

Nevertheless, Mason advised me to talk to Protas. "Before I forget, there's somebody else you ought to talk to about Jackie. He's a loathsome, ghastly creature, and he'll probably lie to you all the time." He was trying again to make me smile. He thought because Martha Graham liked Jackie, Protas might have some insight. Though Mason personally and the company lost money in the lawsuit, Mason could still be lighthearted about Protas. "He construed her will to mean that he owned all her works. He owned her personal property. Her jewelry. Her dresses. Her sideboard. Her sofa." Protas's failure to distinguish between choreography that changed the world and Martha Graham's sofa was the most damning thing Mason had to say about him.

Following George Balanchine's death in 1983, Mason asked Jackie whether he could do a book interviewing everyone who'd danced for Balanchine. When the book was delivered, Jackie told him he had to cut it. Even with edits *I Remember Balanchine* came to more than 600 pages. Mason wanted everyone who'd ever known Balanchine to put their memories on record so that the art wouldn't be lost. Dance is evanescent. Mason was trying to recapture it in encyclopedic detail on the page. He didn't want to go to parties, nor did he like big society fundraisers. He told me he didn't care about "the social shit." He had been moved by what he saw on stage. Though never a dancer or a musician himself, he devoted his whole life to writing and broadcasting about dance so it could move others as well.

When Jackie died, a junior editor at Doubleday called Mason to say the publisher was cancelling the contract for his book on Martha Graham. Possibly *I Remember Balanchine* hadn't sold enough copies to make them anticipate much money from his projected book on Martha Graham. Possibly Jackie had once again exercised her privilege to sign up a book that nobody expected to earn back its costs. It was hard on Mason, though. He'd already invested years in collecting the material for the book. Losing a book that has been in preparation is a little like losing a child. He concealed this from me. I only learned it after Mason's death in 2009 from his assistant Patricia Fieldsteel. He refused to be bitter about it, just as he refused to take offense at Jackie's not being entirely honest with him when she asked him to take her downtown to meet the art house publishers. We said goodbye at the door after lunch. I thanked him, but not very eloquently. His response was more touching than mine. "Well," he said in response to my fumbled words, "she's lucky to have you." I walked out the door half wishing I were writing about him instead of her.

When I was young, I thought class was something that could protect me from bullies. A high-powered university degree, a high-paying job, I thought then, would also remove the insignificance I'd acquired through growing up in Ohio. Mason taught me, instead, that having class was a way of breaking down barriers between people. It was about looking out for other people's anxiousness and knocking down obstacles between you. He made me feel as if it would be wonderful to have lunch with him again, even if I weren't writing a book about someone he knew. He had a painful coughing fit toward the end of our lunch. Before I could express concern, he called over the waiter. He ordered chocolate cake with raspberries for both of us. It was his way of waving away what had just happened. He was conspiring with me. In effect he was saying, now, isn't cake what we were both waiting for? That is how I remember Francis Mason. Whatever critical things there are to say about her, and critical things can be said of all of us, I believe that in cultivating Mason as her friend, Jackie was giving an unmistakable sign of her own perceptiveness and worth. Her class wasn't in her clothes or in her an address on Fifth Avenue. It was in sometimes misleading, but also while she was alive, in sticking by and sustaining a man like him.

8 A Harvard Professor's Wife

Jacqueline Kennedy went officially to India in 1962 with her sister Lee Radziwill. There are photos of them riding on an elephant while wearing heels. It's less well known that Jackie went privately and informally to India several times two decades later. On two of these later occasions she traveled with a Harvard expert on Indian art, Stuart Cary Welch, and his wife Edith. Welch had just died as I was beginning to do the research for my book, but I met and talked to Edith Welch several times. She remembered a side of Jackie that was unusual. Then, quite by accident, she turned her spotlight around and trained it on me.

Stuart Welch, known as Cary, came from a rich family in Buffalo. They owned the newspaper there. As a very young man, he became interested in the art of India and the Middle East. When he went to Harvard in the late 1940s there were no courses in Indian or Islamic art. He had to acquire the specialized knowledge himself. He so impressed the faculty, however, that he was taken on as an instructor and eventually as a curator at Harvard's Fogg Museum. He developed the first Harvard curricula for teaching Indian and Islamic art. His work led to pioneering exhibitions that introduced the art of the Middle East and India to an establishment formerly only interested in the art of Europe or the Americas. He later took on curatorial responsibilities at the Metropolitan Museum of Art in New York in addition to his work on the faculty at Harvard. One of the high points of his career was a 1985 Met exhibition on Indian art from 1300 to 1900. It coincided with an American festival of India arranged by the Indian government. Occasional ill rumors reached me that Welch had sometimes used his publications and museum connections to increase the value of objects in his own private collection. At a Sotheby's sale of his collection after he died, a single page from a Persian miniature, of which he was the leading scholar, sold for over ten million dollars. Much of the remainder of his collection went to Harvard as a gift.

I met Edith Welch in April of 2009 at Youville House, an assisted living facility in Cambridge, Massachusetts. I was told that she might not remember much about Jackie. She had the beginnings of dementia. She'd only recently moved from her own house in Cambridge to assisted living. I knew she was in her late 70s. I spoke to her on the phone after writing her a letter. We agreed to meet for lunch. She sounded fine. I didn't know what to expect when I called for her at the front desk at Youville.

I arrived at the time we'd arranged. She wasn't there. A nurse told me her memory was getting worse. A daughter-in-law from California arrived and was also surprised Edith wasn't there. Nor had I realized that we were going to be three for lunch rather than two. Edith eventually joined us without explanation.

She was small and white haired. She had on a fuchsia cashmere sweater and black trousers. She wore a smart black coat and patent leather shoes. I took one look at her outfit and liked her.

The three of us walked down the street to Darwin's Deli, which was too crowded to sit down. Then we walked around the corner to an Indian buffet. Edith told me that she and her husband had met Jackie through John Kenneth Galbraith, the Harvard economist and Kennedy-era ambassador to India. They had gone to India together at least twice, once in 1979. Another time they landed in what is now Mumbai and travelled to southern India. She thought that on one of these visits Jackie had visited her son, who was traveling in India after he left Brown.

Edith Welch recalled going with Jackie to see some of the sights of Delhi. Jackie was not recognized by the crowds. They went in to see the prime minister. Mrs. Gandhi was angry that they arrived in a battered car. They hadn't been escorted and she insisted that afterwards they must travel in an official car. A new Mercedes stood outside the door when they left Mrs. Gandhi.

Edith also remembered encountering the maharajah of Jaipur. He was called "Bubbles" because so much champagne had been uncorked when he was born. He too was angry Jackie hadn't called to let him know she was coming. Edith believed that Jackie was single-minded in her sightseeing. She wanted to fly under the radar. She didn't want a special car. She didn't aim to do social or political things. Someone objected that Jackie hadn't taken adequately dressy clothes for meeting several of the princely Indian families they called on. She had with her only a single gold jacket for dinner. That was all. There was to be no more couture clothing for riding on elephants. Denim and sunglasses would do.

Jackie had a passion for Indian prints which she began to collect after her first tour of India. Many of the major published sources about Indian art were in her collection when she died. She acquired some art via Galbraith, some later via Welch, and other pieces via his graduate students. Welch was jealous of these graduate students. She had to keep it quiet when she sought help from one who was living in London. Jackie and Cary Welch discussed his writing a memoir of his life for Doubleday. He started on the manuscript before he died. Several months before I met his wife for the first time, he had a heart attack while running to catch a train in Japan. Edith Welch wasn't with him at the time.

Edith remembered a poignant moment when she and Cary were passing through New York on their way to Europe in 1994. Jackie was in the middle of her last illness. They went to see her in her apartment. Edith said hello to Jackie, then excused herself. She went out for a walk around the block so that her husband and Jackie could be together. "Two's company," she told me briskly, "three's a crowd." This was just before Jackie died. Although Edith was related to the Iselins and the Pierreponts, prominent families long established in New York at the end of the nineteenth century, she told me Jackie intimidated her. It was more "my problem than hers," she said.

Jackie had tremendous respect for her husband's learning. Edith tried to stay out of their way. There was also just a hint in what she'd said that Jackie and her husband enchanted one another. This made Edith feel as if she were an unwanted third.

She did remember a humiliating incident from one of their trips to India. Air India offered to upgrade two of their tickets when they arrived at the airport, but not the third. Jackie and her husband sat up in front. Edith resented being the one who had to fly tourist. This was the first time when I wondered whether Jackie and the husband hadn't behaved badly. Oughtn't Jackie to have insisted they all sit in tourist and seen what the airline would have done then? Was sitting in first that important to her? Wouldn't it have been kinder for Edith's husband to take the seat in back? When I told Nancy Tuckerman about this, she said "I can't tell you how unlike Jackie" that would have been. Nancy's memory wasn't perfect. Edith's memory was going too. I include the story here because Edith insisted on it, not as part of a pattern of bad behavior, but as one of the things about Jackie that she could and did remember. Maybe if it did happen, it speaks to Jackie's wanting to be near Welch's scholarship and expertise. That was one of her usual postures in relation to learning. If that were so, Edith couldn't help sometimes feeling left out, especially because long experience of travelling in India made Edith something of an expert herself.

Edith was visibly distressed that she couldn't remember more to tell me. She thought Jackie liked traveling with them because they were relaxed, easy, and not social. When they weren't on the road, they all three sat around not talking and reading their books. That was the best image Edith gave me of Jackie's incognito on the Indian subcontinent.

It was an odd lunch. The daughter-in-law sat with us silently. She never once joined the conversation. I didn't know whether she was there to prevent Edith from saying something compromising, or simply to help out. The next day Edith called me. She suggested our meeting without her daughter-in-law. I wasn't sure what this was about. I thought she'd told me everything she remembered. Nevertheless, we agreed to meet for dinner in a week. I told her I'd bring along the first of the India books Jackie edited at Doubleday. It was a picture book of Indian courtly life. Edith might explain some of the images to me.

This time we walked several blocks to a nicer restaurant where I'd made a reservation in advance. Edith dressed all in black. Again she looked wonderful. She was friendlier on her own. She remembered who I was, though she occasionally repeated things she'd already told me. We sat at a candlelit table and had a glass of wine. The lighting was low. It was almost like a date. We paged through the book on Indian courtly life. I asked her about material from the book I hadn't understood. "What are nautch girls?" I asked her. She said they were originally dancing girls in a maharajah's court, but later in more modern times became nearer to prostitutes. She pointed to an image of women involved in sexual play. "Look at all these girls carrying on," she said without disapproval.

Doubleday published *A Second Paradise: Indian Courtly Life, 1590-1947* to coincide with Welch's 1985 show at the Met. Much of it dwells on courtesans, a higher class of prostitute, above the level of a nautch girl. Rulers of Indian courts who had harems of thirty or forty wives still hired courtesans. They paid large sums for them. They respected them because these women could not be possessed. I wondered whether Jackie identified with courtesans. She had chosen to publish this book, after all. She had chosen to be with three very rich men — JFK, Onassis, and Tempelsman. Had she offered herself to them like an Indian courtesan, a woman who entertained but who refused to be possessed? Edith turned her head to look at me sharply. "You may have something there."

She'd had an interesting life of which I knew only fragments beyond what she'd told me. She'd married Cary Welch in 1954, the year after Jackie married JFK. Instead of going to Acapulco and California as the Kennedys did, the two of them had sailed after their wedding on the *Liberté* for England. From there they'd traveled in the Near East on a working trip. It was certainly more adventure than Jackie had in her early life. Edith wanted to talk to me of what Cambridge used to look like. The tech billionaires with businesses in Kendall Square were buying up the nineteenth-century wooden houses formerly occupied by Harvard professors and grad students. They were rewiring them with security systems that could be monitored from a smart phone. She preferred the scruffiness of Cambridge in the 1960s and '70s.

Edith Welch's cousin, Elizabeth Chanler,

married the travel writer Bruce Chatwin. The Welches sailed up the Maine coast with Bruce and Elizabeth on their honeymoon. Bruce Chatwin, then a budding anthropologist, was as avid as Jackie was for Cary's company. He wanted to be with him as much as possible, even on his honeymoon, to absorb Welch's knowledge. The two women, who lived in their better-known husbands' shadows, kept the show on the road. Bruce Chatwin often lived apart from Elizabeth Chanler but returned to her when he was dying of AIDS. She looked after him until the end. While her husband was organizing one-of-a-kind exhibitions, Edith Welch raised their four children without a smart phone.

We talked of other things. Our dinner came to an end. As I walked her back to her apartment in the retirement facility and we neared the door, she accelerated. She turned and blew me a kiss over her shoulder. Then she disappeared in the door. She reminded me of Liza Minelli refusing to say goodbye to Michael York in *Cabaret*. I tried to keep in touch with her. Several phone calls I left for her at the assisted living facility were not returned.

In the meantime I followed up on an introduction Edith gave me. I talked to a young curator of Indian art at the Met who said that Jackie had surprised Cary Welch. He was known for manipulating his students. He used the power that came from his unassailable position in the art world to control them. He found that he could not manipulate Jackie. She could not be possessed.

I also learned that Cary Welch had affairs with

younger men. When he died in Japan, he wasn't alone. He was traveling with a boyfriend. I decided that was none of my business. Nor was it germane to the Jackie book in any case. Some months later Harvard was sponsoring a gay and lesbian film festival that was open to the public. I was living in Cambridge adjacent to the university. I decided to go. One film was about an American soldier who marries and then goes off to fight in the Middle East. There he discovers his homosexuality. He arrives home to try and come out to his wife and family, though the suggestion is that it's already too late. The damage has been done.

This film had already begun and the auditorium was dark. I was sitting there by myself. Suddenly in the doorway appeared an older woman who searched the audience for a place to sit. It was not crowded. There were maybe thirty people there and seats for thirty more. She came down my row and sat right next to me. I recognized her. "Hello Edith."

She treated it as absolutely normal we should meet again at a gay film festival. "Oh, hello."

We watched the movie together. It was sad at the end, both for the young soldier and his wife. Edith was dry eyed. People around us got up to leave. The organizers turned on the overhead lights to encourage us to leave. She remained sitting where she was. She wanted to talk about the movie. "What did you think?" she asked me. Again she turned her head and gave me a sharp look.

I was embarrassed and still wiping away tears with my knuckles. "Well, it was difficult. The guy was in an awful position."

"You don't know how difficult it is for the woman." She didn't go into details, but I could tell instinctively some of what she'd suffered. She didn't refer to her own situation, but I knew she was speaking of her own marriage. It suddenly made me think of the women I'd dated when I was younger, and my dishonesty with them. I'd never told them about my being unsure of my own sexuality. How many women had I hurt in this way? What damage had I done to them while I was protecting myself? Edith Welch gave me that moment of feeling justifiably ashamed.

One of the characters in E. M. Forster's novel *A Passage to India* remarks that India has a way of bringing you face to face with yourself. In this case it wasn't India that made me catch my image in the mirror. It was the widow of an expert on Indian art, a woman who'd explained courtesans to me, and who'd kept me company one night at a restaurant when I was new in town. I tried again afterwards to call her. Again the call went unreturned. I sent her a copy of my book when it came out, but it wasn't acknowledged. It wasn't like her to be impolite. I think she'd just disappeared into the mists of her darkening memory, but not before she'd shone some light on me.

Spending time with Edith Welch I learned more about Jackie. Yes, she was that gorgeous woman in a beautiful dress up there on top of the elephant, but she was also an academic groupie. She longed for a distinction that came from deep knowledge about arcane subjects. Did she wish to shed the skin of her earlier self who cared too much about clothes and marriage and money? If her youth had been about clothes and photographing marvelously in public, her older years were about going exotic places in private and that single gold jacket shoved almost as an afterthought into her bag. With a few exceptions, she seldom cultivated people like Edith who came from old New England and Newport backgrounds. She was ready to do whatever was necessary to have longterm conversation with Edith's husband. Was there a ruthlessness about the way she dealt with one of the Welches and not the other? Was her pursuit of high culture just as intentional as JFK's of the presidency and Onassis's of his shipping empire? Edith avoided Jackie. She was anyway more modest than Cary Welch about what she had to offer.

Nevertheless, I'm grateful to Edith Welch for this. She gave me a push along the road to self-knowledge. We'd travelled no more than a few blocks together, from assisted living to several restaurants, and back home to Youville after the film festival. The effect on me, though, was as if we'd travelled thousands of miles together in our tourist class seats, hunched down, shoulder to shoulder, talking confidentially in the dark between continents.

About the Author

My previous books have been works of biography, history, and biographical fiction. *Reading Jackie* is a look at the 100 books Mrs. Onassis worked on as an editor. These books reveal her tastes, interests, and even reflections on her own life story. Two cheerful fictions about life inside the Royal Household are *Mrs Queen Takes the Train* and *Prince Harry Boy to Man*. I'm now working on a memoir that mixes literary biography with self-help. *Lord Byron Dared Me to Be Me*. The latest news is on my website: WilliamKuhn.com.

Photograph Credits

Nan Talese, New York, 2009, David Shankbone photographer, via commons.wikimedia.org

Ruth Ansel, New York, 1963, Duane Michals photographer, courtesy of Ruth Ansel

Francis Mason, Princeton, NJ, 2002, courtesy of Patricia Fieldsteel

Edith Welch, Lahore, 1981, with thanks to Arif Rahman Chughtai, courtesy of the Chughtai Museum